What Others Are Saying About *Mayor Frank*...

Steve Imbeau's biography of Mayor Frank Willis is comprehensive and well-documented. It chronicles the various stages in the mayor's life—both professionally and politically—by recounting many of his more substantial accomplishments. But as the narrative unfolds, the reader quickly understands that this isn't simply the story of a career structured around accomplishments. It involves a life spent nurturing, sustaining, and coalescing relationships. A great many of these projects materialized because Frank worked assiduously to cultivate personal friendships with the women and men who would make Florence and the Pee Dee successful. In that regard, Frank's magnanimous personality and his unique ability to convey a unifying vision for the community are the central themes of this book. Steve Imbeau's book captures the essence of those traits superbly.

FRED CARTER,
president of Francis Marion University

Steve Imbeau's writing is well worth the read. He is an engaging and quite clever author. He is bright and his takes on life and history reflect his broad interest in our world. He writes with a southern tone and entertains you as he educates you. You will not go wrong by reading his book, *Mayor Frank*. It outlines an important time in the evolution of Florence from a town to a city, as the infrastructure was built and the culture enhanced to support and encourage city life and growth—all under the leadership and quiet skill of Frank Willis. I came into the administration of McLeod Hospital with much of this work well on its way, helping Mayor Wukela build on the foundation laid for him. I highly recommend this book, which you will enjoy and reread again and again. It also can provide a road map and inspiration to other towns and politicians all over the United States.

E. C. IRVIN,
MD, MBA, FAAFP, and author of *Physicians Should Talk*

I worked with Mayor Frank as the Florence City Manager from 1996 to beyond his term in office. I came to admire his willingness to listen to and meet with anybody and thus build consensus. Mayor Frank was dedicated to the growth of Florence from town to city and started with infrastructure and our city enabling regulations. But he also was eager for outside assistance and help, witness the important role of Hunter Interests Inc. in our work. I was always amazed by the number of projects Mayor Frank could follow and develop, partly because of his keen intellect but also because of his willingness to delegate.

Mayor Frank and Dr. Imbeau have written a fair and balanced history of those days, capturing with stories, details, great photographic memories, and some humor the many accomplishments of our office, our city, and our mayor. Any town, any politician or any administrator can benefit from the timeline and the story artfully told in this book. I think it's a civics class must read.

DAVID N. WILLIAMS,
retired manager of Florence City

MAYOR FRANK

MAYOR FRANK

From Vision to Reality

STEPHEN A. IMBEAU AND FRANK E. WILLIS

credo
house publishers

Published in the United States of America by Credo House Publishers,
a division of Credo Communications LLC, Grand Rapids, Michigan
credohousepublishers.com

ISBN 978-1-62586-207-5

Cover and interior design by Sharon VanLoozenoord
Cover photo by Steve Roos (1998)
Editing by Pete Ford

Printed in the United States of America
First Edition

Library of Congress
Mayor Frank: From Vision to Reality by Stephen A. Imbeau and Frank E. Willis
LCCN 2021904188 (softcover)
Softcover copy placed with the Library of Congress
US Programs, Law, and Literature Division
Cataloging in Publication Program
101 Independence Ave, SE
Washington, DC 20540-4283

Editor's Note
Stephen A. Imbeau has served as a citizen columnist for the *Morning News*
in Florence, South Carolina, since 2013. He has written at least one column
per month since then. All of them have been interesting and informative.
For the record, Stephen has permission from me and the *Morning News*
to publish a collection of his columns that have appeared on the *Morning
News*'s Opinion page. If there is any reason to contact me, I can be reached
at (843) 731-1728 or at *dkausler@florencenews.com*. Regards, Don Kausler
Jr. Editor: *Morning News* (Florence, SC)

CONTENTS

PREFACE

FRANK WILLIS was the mayor of Florence, South Carolina, from 1995 to 2008, just over 13 years, the third-longest-serving mayor of Florence. The city was chartered in 1890 after the 1888 formation of the County of Florence from sections of Darlington and Marion Counties. Both the city and county were named for the daughter of Major Harllee, president of the local railroad, the Wilmington and Manchester.

Mayor Frank grew up quietly in nearby Darlington, graduating from St. John's public high school and attending USC Columbia, graduating in Psychology. Even while in school, he worked for his father in the road construction and site preparation business, Willis Construction, and figured he always would. But Frank discovered along the way that he had a natural knack with people. He is very smart, thoughtful, and quiet, a very good listener, and thus a consensus builder. But consensus is key to the construction business; the quiet organization and concurrence of customers, government agencies, inspectors, suppliers, and subcontractors determines a project's success. The same skills are useful and key in community politics. And so, Frank found as he worked with trade associations, the Florence Rotary Club, and the local economic development groups that the same skill set could translate into friendships and political success.

But Frank had more than an engaging, thoughtful, listening personality. He had a vision, a goal. He wanted to grow Florence with improved infrastructure (probably natural for a road and site contractor) and with regional cooperation. Florence was at a crossroads of sorts. The Florence Civic Center fight was over and the local university, Francis Marion University, was mature and starting to grow;

international and national businesses were noticing Florence and
starting to come to Florence. The community was changing.

Through Rotary friends Grady Greer and Fred DuBard, Frank became involved with the Florence community. The biggest next step
was into economic development through the local economic development support group, Florence County Progress, becoming its chair,
eventually becoming chair of the Florence County Economic Development Authority, and then working to expand the Authority's funding
by creating the Florence County Economic Development Partnership.
Dr. Stephen Imbeau and Mayor Frank basically met through Florence
County Progress; when Frank first became chair of Florence County
Progress, he asked Steve to become his membership chair.

On a parallel track, Frank began a series of meetings to develop
regional consensus across the Pee Dee Region of South Carolina,
working with the South Carolina Office for Economic Development,
who were themselves interesting in fleshing out their then-new concept of regional "economic clusters," a natural fit for Frank.

The next natural step would be election politics, but Frank was
reticent and needed coaxing. This book is about the . . . rest of the
story . . . and success.

Mayor Frank's success is also the story of happening upon opportunity and knowing what to do with it. As William Shakespeare
wrote (*Julius Caesar* 4.3.1599):

"There is a tide in the affairs of men,
which, taken at the flood, leads on to fortune."

Mayor Frank's opportunity: a change in the attitude of Florence
about growth and development symbolized by the new Civic Center, substantial funding potential from the new Drs. Bruce and Lee
Foundation, the significant occurrence of concurring presidents of
Florence Darlington Technical College and Francis Marion University, and a potent group of supporters and advisers.

We believe this book is not only local Florence history but also
instruction for anybody yearning for local leadership and achievement. You need not live in Florence or South Carolina to appreciate
this book, this political education, and this history.

Businessman

FRANK EUGENE WILLIS was born on October 19, 1941, in Bennettsville, South Carolina. He grew up in Darlington, South Carolina, graduating from St. John's High School in 1959, then in 1964 with a degree in psychology from USC Columbia, where he was also a prominent baseball and football player. He next went to the Army Reserves for about a year, then back to Darlington and Florence to work with his father, Eugene (Gene), at Willis Construction Compnay, learning the heavy construction business.

Gene had worked with the Marion, South Carolina-based Hubbard Construction on road construction and site work as a heavy machine operator before going with them to Florida to build bases and barracks for the US Army during World War II. His truck-driving friend Harold Brasington came along; the two became a construction team in Florida. After the war, Hubbard Construction decided to stay in Florida while keeping a small operation in Marion, South Carolina; Hubbard went on to become a major contractor in the Disney Orlando project, completed in 1971.

Harold Brasington returned home after the war and decided to build an auto racetrack in Darlington on land bought from Sherman Ramsey; the sale was agreed to in the course of a poker game, by handshake. Ramsey was a Darlington landowner in the lumber business. The property was about 600 acres, called the DuBose Plantation, bought by the Ramsey family in the 1930s. The deed to the land, initially contingent on a 99-year lease, was exchanged for stock in the new Darlington Raceway Corporation, a very good investment gamble for the Ramseys, as it turned out. Sherman Ramsey was chair of the new company. Before the war, Brasington had raced in the Midwest, racing his own car for small purses, and caught the racing bug. One Ramsey stipulation, that a fishing pond be maintained, led to the unique oval shape of the new asphalt track.

Harold Brasington asked Gene Willis, his construction buddy, to prepare the site and build the track. Willis was able to cobble together the necessary heavy equipment by borrowing equipment the Hubbard Company had left in Marion when they moved to Florida. The racetrack was finished in 1950 and opened to a capacity crowd of about 25,000 people (today it has a capacity of 47,000). The track was 1.25 miles but with steep embankments. The Darlington Raceway remains a NASCAR tradition and nicknames include "The Track Too Tough to Tame" and "The Lady in Black." The track and stands were revised in 1953, 1970, and 1997 and today is at 1.366 miles (367 laps make 501.3 miles); the stands were revised this past decade to compete with growing venues elsewhere on the NASCAR circuit. The 1950 Labor Day weekend race was called the "Southern Five-Hundred" and sponsored by the Central States Racing Association, becoming the next year the "Southern 500" sponsored by the new NASCAR. Darlington is NASCAR's first and oldest commercial racetrack. The 500 Labor Day Weekend race was moved to California and then Georgia from 2004 to 2015; the Darlington race was moved to November until restored to Labor Day (see "NASCAR restores beloved tradition with Darlington's move back to Labor Day," *USA TODAY*, September 2, 2015, and Chancey, S., *The Southern 500*).

Several famous Florentines are associated with the Darlington Raceway including Cale Yarborough, Fred DuBard, and Tom Kinard. The 1990 movie *Days of Thunder* was filmed in part at the racetrack; Florence's Tim Pettigrew, a former Darlington Raceway president, was charged with care and security for the actors. Robert Duval came into Florence to eat and party, and always spoke warmly of the Florence people and his reception. Various Southern 500 commercial sponsors over the years include Heinz, Winston Tobacco, Pepsi, Mountain Due, Dodge Motors, GoDaddy, Showtime, Bojangles, and Cook Out. Transouth Financial, originating in Florence, sponsored an added spring race.

And thus, with a successful major project as a first, a new business was born: Willis Construction concentrated on road building, site preparation, and excavation. Frank got his early construction legs on that project, "helping" his father and learning to be a "water boy." He remembers as an eight-year-old watching in wonder the huge crowds filling the new Darlington Raceway opening in September 1950 on Labor Day. An enormous crowd of 25,000 people filed in that first day, filing surrounding fields and jamming roads for miles. A fascinating detail: the women mostly dressed in their "Sunday Best." The Southern 500 race remains a very important regular circuit NASCAR race, important to both Darlington and Florence. Frank continued to work summers with his father, learning to drive huge Caterpillar Tractor machines at about age 14—before he could legally drive a car.

After returning home from his Army tour and working with his father for about five years, Frank took over Willis Construction in 1970 when his father had a heart attack. The company had grown out of an in-home office in Darlington, moving to space at the accounting offices of Harry Jaillette, then in 1964 to an office trailer parked along Lucas Street in Florence, subsequently to a new office at 821 West Lucas St. Frank had become a licensed small-plane pilot in about 1965 and hoped he could expand the business enough to use a plane for site visits and bidding.

Willis Construction grew and prospered with ups and downs typical of the road construction business. Major projects include some subcontract work on I-95, Burlington Industries plant and building site in Darlington (owned and operated by the Ramsey family), Galey-Lord textiles plant site in Society Hill, the new GE plant site in Florence, the jet runway at the Florence Airport, the Roche Carolina site, and the Honda Way interchange off I-95. Probably the largest project was the 28-mile Conway bypass in cooperation with internationally known Flour-Daniel Construction. Willis Contruction continued to grow with Laddie Hiller then Ron Scott as president, Bruce Smith as treasurer, and Bucky Metts as shop foreman. Bidding six to eight new jobs each week became routine, turning into about $8 million of construction contracts per year.

The construction office remained on Lucas Street in Florence, becoming Frank's nerve center; he often entertained visitors in the back with obligatory cigars. Visitors were impressed by his friendly and ready staff and his tidy desktop; however, he had files carefully stored and cataloged behind him. A clean desktop made it easy for him to lean back and listen. Many city leaders and citizens, from prominent to unnoticed, made the trip to 821 Lucas St. George Jebaily—who actually first met Frank during the campaign from a radio ad, even though both were raised in the area—became particularly fond of his nearly weekly visits to discuss city issues and grow a rich friendship that continues. Jebaily himself would successfully run for city council in 2014 was always an important part of Frank's cadre. Jebaily also energetically worked on Downtown Florence Development and several city center projects and festivals including the famous SC Pecan Festival, now called the SC Pecan Music and Food Festival. George himself narrowly lost a mayor's race in 2020. George was also a regular at the mayor's monthly business roundtable breakfasts.

Unfortunately, Gene Willis was shot in the face one evening in 1974 by an escaped mental patient. He recovered, but ongoing surgeries kept him away from work. Gene later died in 1978.

About 1998, Frank bought Southern Office Supply in Hartsville from founder Cliff Jones, managed by Bruce Smith, who also opened a display at the Florence Airport. Frank closed this business in 2004.

The Associated General Contractors of America (AGC) is the organization of choice for those associated with the construction industry. According to their web page (*acg.org*), AGC "is an organization of qualified construction contractors and industry related companies dedicated to skill, integrity and responsibility. Operating in partnership with its Chapters, the Association provides a full range of services satisfying the needs and concerns of its members, thereby improving the quality of construction and protecting the public interest." AGC established ethics and continuing education for members. Association members subscribe to a monthly report of public projects up for bid with dates and data necessary for informed bids. More information on each project is available online or on-site in the plan room. Project bid opportunities would also come in from architects and construction management companies, or on large projects needing smaller construction companies for supplemental work. Frank and his father worked with AGC from the beginning.

The AGC chapters for North and South Carolina were combined with offices in Columbia, South Carolina, and Charlotte, North Carolina. Starting with the Columbia office, Frank moved on to the Charlotte office to be the president of the Carolinas AGC chapter in 1986. He joined the national AGC board, based in Washington, DC, and worked his way up to be in position to be president as an executive committee member from 1988 and chair of their National Highway Division in 1990, but deferred when he became interested in running for Florence mayor. These organizational experiences taught Frank the value and philosophy of regional cooperation and honed his organizational, people, and political skills.

Public relations for the heavy construction industry are managed by what is called TRIP (the National Transportation Research Nonprofit) based in Washington, DC. According to the TRIP web page, "Founded in 1971, TRIP is a private, nonprofit organization that researches, evaluates, and distributes economic and technical data on surface transportation issues. By generating traditional and social media news coverage, TRIP informs and promotes policies that improve the movement of goods and people, make surface travel safer, and enhance economic development and productivity."

TRIP is intent on promoting general goodwill for road construction, support for public funding of excellent US transportation systems, and ethical standards for the heavy construction industry. Frank became the TRIP President in 1988, having served on the board since 1982. He continued to work with TRIP for many years, even serving as the chair of the Road Information Program from 1990 to 1999. Back in South Carolina, he helped start a similar organization called the South Carolina Transportation Policy and Research Council, originally known as South Carolinians for Better Transportation, serving as its first president from 1980 to 1987.

At about the same time in the early 1980s, Frank also worked with Governors Riley and Campbell on the Commission on Restructuring State Government, helped to write the South Carolina

Transportation Department Plan for Minority Business, and helped
the Committee for Minority Business Enterprise with certification.
He later served again, this time as chair of the South Carolina Transportation Policy and Research Council from 1992.

Frank sold Willis Construction to the CR Jackson Company in
2008, proximate to his final days as mayor. He had begun to scuba
dive in about 1990 and loved to explore clear Caribbean waters; he
loved to travel. In 1999, he married South Carolina's preeminent an-
titrust attorney, Marguerite Smith, putting a smile on his face and
new vigor in his work. The couple loved to vacation in the Grand
Tetons, Washington, DC, and the Caribbean. Frank found time to
play gentleman's golf at the Country Club of South Carolina most
Sunday afternoons with Fred DuBard, Grady Greer, Tom Marschel,
and Dr. Fred Carter, never winning nor losing more than two dol-
lars. After the sale of Willis Construction, he also began a construction and bidding consulting business called Willis Consulting. Frank
was honored by the Florence Chamber of Commerce as the Small
Busines Person of the Year in 2009. He later moved back to economic
development in 2012—this time with the County of Darlington.

While still working in the construction business, Frank began
community service with the Rotary Club (Four-Way Test Award in
1997), the local BB&T Bank board, the YMCA (Distinguished Service
Award in 1983), the Leukemia Society, the Winthrop College Advi-
sory Board, the Francis Marion University Foundation Board, and
of course Florence County Economic Development Authority. Frank
became Mr. Economic Development in Florence and the region.
Frank first worked with the support group called Florence County
Progress, then the Florence County Economic Development Authority where he helped to guide the landing of the significant Roche
Carolina plant in Florence, along with Mayors Rocky Pearce and
Haigh Porter, Senator Hugh Leatherman, and Governor Campbell.
He became the authority chair in 1991. He facilitated the arrival of
the energetic Michael G. Barnes as Florence's first certified economic
development director. In 1994, Frank's last full year as authority
chair, unemployment stood at 5.7 percent (down from over 8 percent), retail sales up 6 percent to $2.8 billion including 24 new retail
businesses or shops, airport enplanements up 20 percent, and four

major big business expansions including the Phase II expansion at Roche Carolina. Frank resigned from the Authority to run for mayor. But even once mayor of Florence, Frank continued to work hard to transform the Authority into the Partnership with combined county and private business backing with the energetic support of Emerson Gower from the power company and Don Herriott at Roche Carolina; thus, economic development gained political clout and private business "buy-in," yet still closely aligned with the county. This important transformation of Florence County Economic Development Authority work, financial support, and politics was finalized by State Charter in 1996 and fully functional by 1999. In later years, Frank would carry this model to the County of Darlington, his old home.

Frank was awarded the key to the City of Florence in 1984, the National Rebuild America Award in 1985, the Southeastern Economic Developers Association Volunteer of the Year Award in 1992, and the South Carolina Ambassador Award for Economic Development in 1993. He was awarded the Doctor of Humanities degree from Florence Marion University in 2008. He continued to serve with the North Eastern Strategic Alliance (see "NESA" chapter) from its founding in 2000 until 2012.

Mayor Frank has been many things to many people, but his longest and most respected relationships have been that of his employees and family; sometimes his employees *were* family.

Most employees worked for Willis Construction for 20 to 30—or even 40—years, and it wasn't unusual for multiple family members to be employed at one time or another. It was this feel of "family" and the respect with which Frank treated his employees that kept them there for so long. He knew them well and cared about them all.

Throughout his political tenure, he always had time for his employees. One thing Frank did that added to the respect of his employees was he conducted most of his mayoral business from his office at Willis Construction. This effectively offered two major advantages: it kept him close and visible to his employees, and it allowed his office staff to get to know his constituents so that they could better serve them together. As most of his decisions were, it was another good one. One result of this decision came when Frank learned of the need for a literacy program among his employees and arranged for classes to be held on-site to better accommodate their needs. It was a huge success.

Another example came when, during his first campaign, Frank met an elderly lady who lived in fear every day. As it happened, her home was surrounded by overgrown, abandoned lots that harbored illicit activity. One of the first things Frank did as mayor was recruit some of his own employees and equipment to clean out the lots all around hers and make her feel safe again (see "Drug Free Florence" chapter). The joy this lady felt could only be measured against the joy Willis Construction employees who volunteered to help her felt. This was yet another kind of effort that endeared Frank to others and always made him so approachable.

More blessed than anyone to have Frank in their lives would be his family, particularly his mother and youngest siblings. When Gene died, Frank inherited the role of taking care of the family. Though not a role any young man would look forward to, Frank did it with apparent ease and slid naturally into his father's shoes. Throughout all of his accomplishments, hard work, and political growth, there was a man who was there for his family . . . offering advice, supporting, encouraging, and forever listening. Most of all, he set an example—and if you ask either of his siblings, they will both say there never was a better one.

The Campaigns

FRANK WILLIS did not aspire to be a politician. He was a highway contractor and businessman. He, of course, worked with local politicians in his business and when he was appointed to and then moved up in Florence County Progress and the Florence County Economic Development Authority. While he did not study politics in school nor run for political office until he ran for mayor of Florence, he turned out to be a natural. He was handsome, good with people although a bit reticent, thoughtful, and well-spoken, the sort of person who considers carefully what he is going to say, but in a natural not forced or arrogant way; and he had a winning smile. And he was a great listener. The construction business had taught him how to build consensus.

Sometime in late 1994, Florence Mayor Haigh Porter decided not to run for reelection. And so, the search began among the political parties for candidates, although neither party had particular organizational strength in Florence at that time. Frank's success in economic development and his membership in the Monday Rotary Club attracted the attention of some civic and business leaders who decided to pursue him. Rocky Pearce was mayor before Haigh Porter and was interested in running again and had support in the Democratic Party; John Chase, who was from a prominent Florence family and currently on the city council, was interested in running on the Republican ticket. Frank's friends thought this could be Frank's time.

In early January 1995, some friends invited Frank to meet with them after a Chamber of Commerce luncheon at the Florence Area Civic Center; the group included Joe Turner, Robert Williams, Fred DuBard, Grady Greer, and shortly thereafter, Pam Osborne. Fred and Grady lead the effort. They urged him to run for election as mayor of Florence. Frank was surprised and flattered, but he needed time to think; also, he was concerned that he had no way to raise money or voter support given that 1) he was new at politics and 2) the Democratic Primary was less than two months away, in February. As he told them: "I've never run for public office before, never even considered running for office. I don't know if anyone would vote for me. I don't know what it would cost to run for mayor. Show me that there will be some support for me out there and we'll talk about it" (*Greater Pee Dee Business Journal*, December 1998). The initial group soon invited him to a meeting at the DuBard Inc. conference room with about 40 people from all over the community who told him: we represent the community, and we will support you. We will donate money to you, and we will get out the vote for you.

Frank made his decision: "Yes." He decided to compete in the Democratic Primary, even though he was not registered with either party.

Frank then threw himself very seriously into the race. Pam Osborne managed the early part of the campaign on a very thin budget; there really was no money except that provided by Fred DuBard and Frank. Pam organized picnics, community coffees, and barbecues at places like Red Doe Plantation to raise some money. Willis Construction employees in logo shirts went door to door as Frank himself did, in both black and white neighborhoods, often doing acts of kindness along the way, never to be forgotten.

Through his friendship with Rick Silver of the prominent Columbia, South Carolina, Chernoff-Silver Public Relations and Political Consultant firm, Frank was put in touch with Reba Hull as a potential campaign manager. Reba was experienced and deft at politics and organization, having just served as press secretary first for Representative Robin Tallon and then South Carolina Lieutenant

Governor Nick Theodore. Frank hired Reba as his campaign manager after a meeting at the Florence Airport. Reba moved back and forth from Columbia to Florence during the campaign, spending most of her time in Florence.

The campaign was successful, and Frank defeated Rocky Pearce in the Democratic Primary on February 28, 1995, by 1,911 votes to 1,228. He also raised about $70,000, a good amount for that time. Fred DuBard was chair of the advisory committee and Grady Greer chair of the finance committee.

Frank ran a classic, old-fashioned small-town political campaign. He connected with business leaders in banking, real estate, insurance, and the professions; he connected with "big business" folks; he connected with the educational community; he connected with the middle class; and he connected with the ethnic communities, particularly in the Greek and black communities, even though Rocky Pearce had previous support among the major ethnic leadership.

Frank walked door to door all over the city—both black and white neighborhoods and both Democrat and Republican strongholds. He attended fundraisers put together by folks like Joe Turner, Robert Williams, Grady Greer, and Fred DuBard. He attended coffee clutches and community forums. Frank made special efforts to include the black community in his campaign; he promised no more racially split votes on the city council.

The general election was run much the same as the primary: grassroots and door-to-door. Frank maintained his "man of the people" image. Frank also had a specific platform: clean up the drug-infested areas, make Florence an All-American City once again, expand and improve infrastructure, revitalize downtown Florence, and improve economic development with a regional approach.

There is a great story that captures the essence of Frank's grassroots campaign. One afternoon, walking alone door-to-door in a heavily Republican neighborhood, he rang a doorbell. A nine-year-old girl answered, Brittany. Frank asked, "Is your mother home?" Brittany responded, "Yes, Mr. Willis, she is coming right now." A surprised Frank could only ask, "How does she know who I am?" and the mother responded, "Well, Mr. Willis, she watches the news and sees you on TV; she knows you are an owner of a construction business and now running for mayor of Florence. In fact, she wants us to vote for you." Frank was astonished and thanked them for their support and attention. As he walked to the neighbor's house, Brittany ran after him and said, "Mr. Willis, we want one of your yard signs." Frank tells her that his car is a long way away, but he will get one later, and bring it to them. Well, about an hour later, he comes back with the yard sign and Brittany is patiently waiting on the front porch with hammer in hand, ready to pound the sign into the ground. A sign from heaven—Frank now knew he could win this election. Brittany held the Bible at Frank's swearing in and came to the All-American City finals in Kansas City. She went on to college and then pharmacy school in Charleston. Brittany and Frank stay in touch.

Frank defeated Mayor Chase on May 8, 1995, with 3,517 to 1,937 votes to become the next mayor of Florence.

Frank was reelected as mayor of Florence in 2000 and 2004 without opposition from either party. By 2006, he had a substantial and deep base in Florence and had name recognition throughout the region, representing about 25 percent of the state. So, he decided to run in the Democratic Primary for governor against Tommy Moore, C. Dennis Aughtry, and Kenneth Holand (Holand dropped out before the election). Tommy Moore won by a 2:1 margin over Frank in solid second place (Tommy about 372,000 votes and Frank about 195,000 votes). Tommy Moore lost in November; Republican Mark Sanford was reelected as governor. Frank's gubernatorial campaign was managed by Carey Crantford of the Crantford Research Firm. Frank's wife, Marguerite Willis, also played a major role as surrogate speaker.

Frank's reelection as mayor in 2008 did not go well; the political fates seemed to line up against him. Frank faced for the first time a Democratic challenger, Stephen Wukela, a trial attorney with a powerful father in the local and state Democratic Party. Stephen had previously run for the senate and lost against multi-term incumbent Senator Hugh Leatherman, the Republican chair of the South Carolina Senate Finance Committee. However, he gained name recognition and kudos for the bravery (or foolishness) of opposing a member of Florence's political establishment. Frank was now the third-longest serving mayor in the history of Florence, only bested by David McLeod and Herbert Gilbert. But Stephen Wukela was a key local supporter of the popular Senator Barack Obama while Frank and Marguerite supported Senator Hillary Clinton in that year's Democratic Primary for US President; the presidential primary was on the same ballot as the mayoral primary.

Well, Frank felt he would do well anyway and ran a low-key campaign, in part because of the Senator Obama factor, since Mayor Frank did not want to unnecessarily stir up any black vote against himself in the city election. Unfortunately, the local parties decided that the Republican and Democratic primaries would both be moved from spring to fall with the presidential primaries, be held on the same day, and that an individual voter could only vote in one of them. Frank's strategy almost worked anyway, but a Republican gremlin was also at work against Frank.

A controversial Republican city councilman was on the Republican Primary ballot and many of Frank's key Republican and Independent supporters voted in the Republican Primary, assuming Frank would do just fine on the Democratic side since they wanted to turn the controversial Republican out of office. If they had at all guessed at the Democratic Primary's outcome, they would have voted in the Democratic Primary for Frank, and Frank would have won handily. But he lost by the incredible low count of just *one vote*. One vote. An automatic municipal recount upheld Wukela's narrow victory. Citing "voter confusion," Frank appealed the recount to the South Carolina Democratic Party, who ruled in favor of Wukela and denied the mayor's request for another primary election. As usual, there were contested ballots, more for Stephen than for Frank, so Frank went to court. Frank took the matter before a local circuit court, but the judge dismissed the case and stated that the results from the Democratic Primary were legitimate. Frank then appealed the circuit court's decision to the South Carolina Supreme Court, but the case was similarly dismissed.

After the Supreme Court decision, Frank conceded the race, telling the *Florence Morning News*: "It's over." The Republicans had fielded no candidate for mayor since many of them supported Frank and assumed he would win the Democratic Primary. Former Mayor Pearce came in as a write-in candidate for mayor, and worked hard,

but was certainly the underdog; Stephen Wukela won the final
election by about 10 percentage points and became Florence's new
mayor in 2008.

Historical and editorial assistance came from Barbara Sylvester, Pam Osborne,
and Reba Hull.

Drug Free Florence

IMAGINE FEARING your own front porch because cocaine dealers roam from nearby vacant lots. Now imagine the scene changing in one short day of shared labor. A neighborhood grandmother told Frank after a successful lot clearing, with tears in her eyes, "Mayor Frank, this is the first time in nine years I have felt safe sitting on my front porch. Thank you so very much." The Mayor's Initiative for a Drug Free Florence empowered citizens to work with neighbors and city police to reclaim their community.

A general sense of powerlessness seemed to have gripped both police and citizens alike by 1994 or so. Neither, acting alone, could adequately address the problems of escalating crime and drug use. The police had neither the equipment nor the finances to address the entire issue, and individual citizens often feared confronting criminals. As a result, hoodlums had overtaken some vacant and overgrown lots, establishing lookouts and booby traps of nail boards and broken bottles to ensnare police or provide warning. In some of the worst neighborhoods, crime was growing nearly 3 percent annually. Elsewhere, neighborhoods were growing apart as acts of robbery and violence created fear and suspicion. Any nearby convenience stores lost customers who increasingly feared stopping at a store where drug runners huddled around the public pay phone. This general feeling eventually led to citizen reaction.

A convenience store and Dilmar Oil gas station on South Church Street complained about an adjacent lot owned by the state that was overgrown with kudzu and had become a place for teenagers to harass nearby cars stopped at the traffic signal . . . and to harass store customers. That was Frank's first lot clearing. The process took some time and energy: 1) identify the owners, 2) get permission, 3) get clearing permits, 4) clear the lot, and 5) haul off the debris to the landfill. The city could do numbers 1, 2, 3, and 4; Frank would do number 4, sometimes personally with Willis Construction equipment. For this first lot clearing on South Church Street, Frank drove the equipment and backhoe himself. Dilmar then contributed to building a small police substation nearby and the important gas station was safely back in business.

Jones Park in north Florence was a similar situation, but the Brothers and Sisters Unit for One Cause were fed up with criminals; Mother Catherine Fulton was particularly energized. With the help of the local Jaycees, the Unit organized the Northside Anti-Drug Coalition and held an event in Jones Park in early May 1995. Pastors and local leaders such as councilman Billy Williams joined in. Fulton explained, "It's about the kids. We must protect our kids." Near Timrod Park in central Florence, a random act of violence that left one person paralyzed sparked that neighborhood to mobilize. The criminals were active all across the city; the whole city was ready for change.

Newly elected, Mayor Frank Willis went to Police Chief Ralph Porter, asking simply, "What can I do?" The chief highlighted the problems found in vacant lots, and soon, with landowner permission in hand, Willis Construction private machinery was bulldozing the areas. In another area, a string of daytime burglaries spurred action. As citizens moved, the police and city stood ready to support with advice, manpower, and at times, money. In the end, the communities realized they had been constantly reacting in fear to crime and began acting positively to prevent it.

The mayor quickly moved to announce the Mayor's Initiative for a Drug Free Florence and a Red Ribbon Task Force. The mayor wrote an important letter that was published in the *Morning News* on August 14, 1995:

"The Community can fight city drug problem.

Thirty years ago when I first moved to Florence, I was introduced to a friendly, up and coming community with just the right mix of small town southern hospitality and progressive business opportunity. Most people knew each other or knew someone in the family. Neighbors pulled together to help out in times of need, and over the years pride in the "Magic City" of Florence grew proportionally to the rapid development of new jobs and industry. Today we see a Florence that has changed, evolving with the times—mostly for the better. New houses, schools and shopping centers dot the landscape, testifying to the strength of our local economy and the quality of life lived here. We can attract, and have attracted, top notch, high tech industry. Our medical community is second to none. We are poised on the verge of the 21st Century to become a strong force in shaping the future of South Carolina. The residents of Florence have many reasons to be proud of their accomplishments.

But for us to flourish, we have to be honest with ourselves about our problems—problems that are hard to face and even harder to solve. Since my campaign for mayor, I have taken a guided tour through abandoned houses rigged with booby traps designed to maim or injure anyone trying to get into a drug dealer's hideout. I have spoken to an elderly lady who is afraid to leave her house for fear that hoodlums will enter her house looking for money . . . again. And our jail is full of underaged drug offenders who buy and sell drugs as easily as you or I buy ice cream cones.

Those of us who focus on the future of Florence cannot overlook all this. School teachers, business owners, ministers and families all have a very real interest in stopping the drug abuse problem here in Florence. Simply put, we all have a stake in making Florence drug-free. To this end, I am committing my energy to rally the efforts of the public and of private business to deter the drug abuse problem. I am asking people from all over the city to join the Mayor's Task Force for a Drug Free Florence. North, East, South and West will join with a special directive: To reduce the use and distribution of illicit drugs in our city. I have called on some very capable individuals to coordinate the effort and I have every confidence in their ability as leaders to help find solutions to this complex problem.

Drug abuse is not simply a government problem or law enforcement problem. It is a community problem. Only the will, desire and perseverance of our community will drive the dealers and users out of Florence.

We as a community must take a stand and send a strong message that we will no longer tolerate the insidious disease that infects our Community. With the Community as the leader, law enforcement officials can and will do their part. Together we can become Drug Free Florence." Signed, Mayor Frank Willis.

Folks from the Unit, other north Florence citizens, Circle Park Prevention Center, the Coalition for Alcohol and Drug Abuse, the police department, the sheriff's department, and the Task Force of Communities all joined in. A Drug Free Florence Fund was established to raise money. The original steering committee included Frank Willis, George White, Carolyn Pusser, and Catherine Fulton. The formal task force was chaired by Catherine Fulton and Carolyn Pusser assisted in finance by Robert Williams (Pee Dee Electric) and Miriam Baldwin (McLeod Medical Center); also, Rick Putnam, Olivia Joe, and Yulundra Heyward were critical volunteers. The task force collected nearly $13,000 in donations, plus city equipment and the coordinated labor of neighbors and residents. The effort was multi-pronged: 1) physically clear empty, overgrown lots and remove derelict housing, 2) start neighborhood watch groups, and 3) put police into known drug use or drug sales areas of the city. Many volunteers and city employees worked on executing the project:

Circle Park Prevention Center (a hundred volunteers)
The City of Florence Public Works Department (10 folks and
    heavy equipment)
The Coalition to Prevent Juvenile Crime (10 folks to promote
    the project)
The Florence Police Department (10 folks)
Willis Construction (10 folks plus equipment)

Lot clearing was in full swing by October of 1995.

A rich collaboration of the city's cultures made this project an ongoing success story. To encourage participation in the beginning, some 17,000 copies of "Citizen's Guide to Stopping Illegal Activities" were distributed to every Florence household via volunteers and the public works department. The police placed advertisements on the local government-access cable television channel and released weekly news releases to local newspapers, on signs posted by neighborhood associations, and in neighborhood newsletters. A Citizen Police Academy was established, and some 210 people had already participated in its weekly class offerings or scheduled meetings by 1997. Police inexperience and community suspicion initially slowed the Neighborhood Association creation process. But each of these two groups taught the other, creating appreciation among officers of the community policing concept and among citizens for the police's limitations.

Aggressive follow-up to citizen requests and recruitment of the community into police operations, including public forums on accreditation and the permanent assignment of officers to communities, has established mutual trust and respect. When the call came to clear lots in blighted areas, residents in the predominantly minority neighborhood were joined by white and black doctors, executives, police, and clergy in the successful effort to reclaim their community.

In the first three years, the effort reclaimed 51 overgrown lots marked as eyesores and drug havens. Nearly one hundred acres had been reclaimed by 1997—mainly by one-day clearing parties—freeing police officers for patrols elsewhere. With less time spent reacting to crime, officers now help community groups prevent crime.

The police department was able to reorganize its 89 members for permanent assignment within neighborhoods. Complementing that, 17 neighborhood associations—making up one-third of the city—now meet regularly with officers, having matured from small groups of worried families into influential bodies of genuinely concerned citizens. The police department won accreditation (the Commission on Accreditation of Law Enforcement Agencies) in 1996 for meeting 370 nationally recognized performance standards, only the ninth local South Carolina law enforcement agency to do so.

Statistically, Florence's citywide crime dropped 9 percent in the
first two years of the program and in the worst areas by 85 percent.
At least one hundred acres of former blight were put back into the
community. In the once-besieged convenience store, business went
up, 10 jobs were preserved, and reported local crimes were down
nearly 40 percent—even though crime reports are more likely with
the new substation.

The successful initiative against drug use and sales improved
community confidence, provided the city some insulation from
civil litigation, and would ultimately reduce citizens' insurance
premiums. More difficult to measure but perhaps more valuable,
Florence residents reconnected to their city and each other. Florence's National Night Out against crime drew some 1,100 people, one of South Carolina's largest gatherings. The neighborhood
associations blossomed from a single group to 17 organizations
united by an overarching Neighborhood Council, which the
mayor began to coordinate between associations and the police.
The associations receive monthly crime reports from the police
and unite neighborhoods through regular meetings, newsletters, and, in at least one, a computer lab with a daily after-school
study hall. In some neighborhoods, property values increased as
crime decreased.

The police department's improved accreditation gave confidence
to citizens and officers alike that citizen issues will be handled
fairly and professionally. Police job turnover decreased, and the department's internal satisfaction increased. Overall satisfaction with
the department rose, evidenced by a 44 percent decrease in citizen
complaints over the previous year. In general, the community has
come to "own" the process and the results.

This chapter is adapted in part from the Florence All-American City & Community
Award application of 1997, written by Trip DuBard. Historical and editorial assistance
came from George Jebaily and Commander Anson Shells.

All-American City & Community Award Campaign

FRANK'S TRUE passion was the quality of life in Florence. One reason people took to him during his campaigns was that his passion resonated with them; Florence was a great place to live, and he could, together with them, make it even better. The All-American City & Community Award is an honor with prestige, but it also symbolizes a great spirit of togetherness, energy, and quality; it is attached to only a $10,000 stipend, so the money is not the important feature. Frank knew that All-American City was a major campaign plank; plus, its implementation, win or lose, would provide spark and energy and synergy in the city.

All-American City has been sponsored by the National Civic League since 1949; the League itself dates to 1894 and lists President Teddy Roosevelt among its founders. Funding is also provided by the Allstate Foundation. Ten awards are made each year with the top 30 cities coming together for a two-day competition and judging. Florence last won an award in 1965 under Mayor David McLeod. There are 10 areas of interest including resident participation, community leadership development, government performance, volunteerism and philanthropy, intergroup relations, civic education, capacity for cooperation and consensus building, community vision and pride, and regional cooperation. Each city applicant must address all and be prepared to present three specific projects to the judges. The judges want demonstration projects that are civic, collaborative, inclusive, and important. In 1997, they hoped to see cities exhibit interest in vulnerable boys and men.

As the new mayor, Frank started to work right away on All-American City. He viewed it as an important way to unite the city and substantiate his election campaign promises to win both black and white support and to stop the recent tradition of divided votes by color on the city council. By the fall of 1996, the city had established by ordinance the All-American City Steering Committee, chaired by Pam Osborne with members including Frank Willis, David Wansley, Ed Robinson, Barbara Sylvester, Carrington Baker, Charlene Hewett, Jim Briggs, Tom Kinard, Trip DuBard, Pat Northern, Barbara Brooks, Tom Truitt, Tom Ewart, George Alley, Herbert Ames, Bill Bradham, Sandy Durant, Katy Rogers, Jack Schuller, Doris Lockhard, Dorothy Hines, David Williams, Jane Pigg, and Stephen Imbeau. In January 1997, the committee began to solicit projects for review. On March 27, three were selected for the application submission, mostly written by Trip DuBard: the Pee Dee Partner in Education Program, the Drug Free Florence Initiative, and the Carver Community Center.

On April 22, Florence was selected out of 119 applicants as one of 30 to go up to the next level—to the Final All-American City competition in Kansas City, Missouri. The competition included cities from California, Colorado, Connecticut, Illinois, Indiana, Iowa, Kansas, Maryland, Massachusetts, Missouri, New York, North Carolina, North Dakota, Ohio, Oregon, South Carolina, Texas, and Virginia. Excitement was in the air and trumpeted in the *Morning News* editorials: Florence was on its way to All-American City!

The steering committee opened an office downtown donated by Francis Marion University (FMU) at 309 West Evans St. The committee began to develop the three presentations, raise money to help pay for travel and hotel space, and solicited pictures of Florence landmarks old and new from the community to use in the presentations. Frank was hopeful that teenagers would be able to go to Kansas City to support the presentations. Next came a unifying slogan from a contest sponsored by the newspaper. Three winners presented the winning slogan, "Share the Vision . . . Feel the Magic," which was put on T-shirts, bumpers, binders, stickers, etc. . . .

The three projects demonstrated Florence's ability to work together to identify and then solve a community problem. First, the Educational Project featured Pee Dee Education Foundation with Florence 1 Schools building a partnership between business and education to mentor at-risk students, provide teachers with additional funding, and increase the number of high school students going on to college. The Chamber of Commerce was key to the project, enlisting businesses in the tutoring program and preparing students to take the SAT. (The presentation was managed by Tom Truitt, Tom Ewart, and David Wansley.) The second project, the Carver Project, offered alternative school-based health care, a health center assisted by McLeod Regional Medical Center and the South Carolina Department of Health and Environmental Control (SC DHEC), and adult education from Poynor School and Head Start for early childhood. (The presentation was managed by Barbara Brooks and Willie Mayshack.) The final project was the Mayor's Initiative for a Drug Free Florence, boasting 51 cleared buildings or lots mostly by Willis Construction and community efforts to reduce drug and alcohol usage by Circle Park Behavioral Center and the Coalition for Alcohol and Drug Abuse Prevention. (The presentation was managed by Frank Willis.)

And so off Florence goes to Kansas City with at least 30 folks by bus. Travelers included Mitizi Adams, Robert Adams, A.C. Agnew, George Alley, Herbert Ames, Carrington Baker, Bill Bradham, Jim Briggs, Barbara Brooks, Carolyn Butler, Bill Burr, Ngukkia Gannon, Emily Clark, Winfied Cullins, Corey Davis, Martha Davis, Nina Davis, Sherman Davis, Vanessa Davenport, Trip DuBard, David Durant, Sandy Durant, Tommy Edwards, Cucie Ervin, Carla Ervin, Charlie Ervin, Larson Ervin, Teresa Ervin, Cultive Fulton, Carolyn Garbrell, Jerry Garbrell, Choka Godbolt, Dr. Harold Gowdy, Ashby Gower, Les Heavener, Charlene Hewitt, Avery Hewitt, Dorothy Hines, Murray Hines, Stephen Imbeau, Pam Jarmon, George Jebaily, Will Jones, Ben Johnson, Tim Kauffman, Brian Kelley, Tom Kinard, Jade Kurlan, Brittany Lanford, Marsha Lanford, Doris Lockhard, Josefina Arquana, Larry Mathews, Wilma Matthews, Bernard McDaniel, Pam

McDaniel, Jay Nathan, Neal Nathan, Raj Nathan, Mickey Northern, Pat Northern, Pam Osborne, Jane Pigg, Kate Purvis, Rick Putnam, Ed Robinson, Robert Ross, Jack Schuler, Marshall Smith, Barbara Sylvester, Shirley Thomas, Anita Williams, Billy Williams, David Williams, Grace Williams, Kim Williams, Robert Williams, Leah Williams, Frank Willis, Netta Whisenhunt, Jean Zollcoffer, and Murray Jordan.

The weekend of June 5–7 at the Kansas City Hyatt Regency Hotel was busy, but also fun for the Florence contingent. Opening night featured a cookout in Penn Valley Park; the next day there was a great picnic at Liberty Park with its World War I National Museum and Monument. On Friday and Saturday, many folks toured the Harry S. Truman Presidential Library, his summer home, and the old Pony Express offices in nearby St. Joseph.

Tom Kinard hosted his normal Florence "Kinard 'N Coffee" radio show on Friday morning, but the Kansas City time was 5 a.m.; the special four-hour broadcast was supported by an astonishing 44 companies back home. That Thursday night, at dinner, someone asked Tom what would make him speechless on the air, and he responded "Well, if all the ladies would show up in pajamas, no makeup, and hair askew." Bright and early the next morning with Tom live on the air, in walks Pam Osborne, Carrington Baker, Charlene Hewitt, and Barbara Sylvester in pj's—much to the amusement of the other guests and to Tom's amazement and surprise. He was speechless.

The All-American City interviews and presentations stretched out over two days. Tom Kinard and Jim Briggs did much of the Florence presentation work, with a video presentation written by Trip DuBard and produced by the combined efforts of WPDE and WBTW. The final presentations were only allowed 10 minutes each, and Tom Kinard spoke for Florence. The judges mingled among the audience, hoping to get a flavor of the normal folks (they had also physically visited the final 30 cities in the past several weeks).

The awards banquet was all glitter and Florence was full of anticipation. But "Florence" was not called. Florence had lost and was not named All-American City for 1997. The ride home was weary and quiet. But Florence had come together, Florence had produced a great product, and Florence had made a great impact on Kansas City, as Florentines of all colors and political parties overcame the opposition and lost in style. Black people and white people cried together and rode the long road home together.

Florence applied several more times for the award but did not again make the "final 30."

And so . . . the world turns. And Frank Willis . . . Frank kept on moving ahead.

Historical and editorial assistance came from Trip DuBard, Barbara Sylvester, Pam Osborne, and Tom Kinard.

Preventing Juvenile Crime

EVEN BEFORE going to the All-American City competition, it was obvious to Frank and the city leadership that race relations were amiss in Florence, even though a narrowly predominantly African American city. And so once back home, the mayor was determined to "do something about it." Not because Florence had lost in Kansas City, or wanted to win a future competition, but because it was the right thing to do, and now was the time to do it.

As early as Frank's inauguration, a small conversation group of church and synagogue folks had already begun to meet in small groups calling themselves "Face Up"; early key leaders were Eric Heiden, Elder Williams, Grace Duncan, Fred Reese, James Littles, Stephen Wukela, George Jebaily, and Ruth Smith. After growing to about 50 individuals, they joined in with the Palmetto Project in mid-1976. The Palmetto Project was a statewide race relations and homeless advocacy group started back in 1973 by Steve Skardon, former *Florence Morning News* reporter and former aid to the National Democratic Convention Committee.

Even before going to Kansas City, Mayor Frank met with several advisers and leadership in the Florence black community including Reverend Diggs, Freddie Jolley, Freddie Williams, Reverend

McCutcheon, Reverend Alexander, and others. Later, they started larger meetings open to the general public, called "Building Bridges" and "People to People," in several local school auditoriums. But the causes of racial disparities and mistrust went deeper and wider than individual relationships.

The upshot was a formal request to the city council by Freddie Jolley in mid-July 1997 to launch a biracial task force to begin racial discussions and bridge building. The Mayor's Human Relations Committee was begun. By the end of July 1997, Frank appointed 16 folks to the new committee: Reverend Diggs (also later Reverend Alexander), Reverend Mack Hines, Henry Peoples, Robert Grooms, George Jebaily, David Williams (city staff), Sandy DuRant, Mary Bowman, Timothy Waters, Freddie Williams, Dathon Reynolds, William Deberry, Frank Willis, Tricia Caulder, Lenda Hearon, and Richard Harrington—these were later joined by Elliott Franks, Cleveland Thomas, Kent Caudill, Chuck Whipple, and the mayors of Timmonsville and Lamar. The original mission statement (not adopted until June 1998) read: "The Mission of the Mayor's Human Relations Committee is to bring our culturally diverse communities together for the purpose of building unity, of promoting economic growth, and of development in all sectors of our community. The committee will address problems that cause disparity and disharmony between community members. The committee will build relationships to enhance the respect and dignity of every citizen and to enhance the betterment of the entire community. The committee will accomplish all this by promoting community dialogue, economic opportunity emphasizing the underdeveloped communities, grassroots leadership, and neighborhood improvement working with both the government and private business."

A major town hall meeting called "Building Bridges" was scheduled for November 10, 1997, to be carried on live commercial television WIS-10 TV, anchored by David Stanton; Governor David Beasley was invited. About 300 people attended to discuss economic barriers and opportunities, race relations, and education. Reverend Mack Hines summed up the night: "We've come here tonight to talk to each other, not at each other. This is the beginning point tonight and I think we are on the right road."

The groups coordinated on the construction of a city-owned and -managed skateboard park in west Florence within the McLeod Park baseball facility in late 1997, using a combination of city money ($24,000) and money raised by Joe Lewis ($16,000). The new park was supported at a city council meeting on June 16, 1997, by dentist Eric Heiden, photographer Joe Lewis, and the Human Relations folks, including Freddie Jolley. The park has recently been refurbished.

By the end of 1998, the committee members shifted a bit to be led by Reverend Terry Alexander (chair), Rabbi Marc Kline (vice-chair), and Mona Lisa McCray (secretary), with members George Jebaily, Buquilla Ervin, Dr. Paul Vivian, Pat Gibson-Hye Moore, Annie Brown, Dr. Harold Gowdy, Dr. Jim Allen, Sandy DuRant, Trisha Caulder, Timothy Waters, James Williams, Deitra Reese, Peter Lee, Richard Harrington, Valencia Butler, Frank Willis, and Richard Harrington. Six or seven community meetings were held in 1998, often sponsored by private businesses; steps were taken to include African Americans in city appointments and industry councils. Even by the end of 1997, several students were already enrolled in employment training programs; literacy work at Florence 1 Schools was beefed up. Grant applications were begun, including "Investing in Healthy Communities" for $5,000 from the State of South Carolina; some funding from GE was in the pipeline.

In 1999, the committee joined with the City of Florence, the Florence Police Department, and Florence 1 Schools to support the new City of Character campaign. City of Character chose a key word or phrase each month, emphasized on billboards, bus stops, and city literature, including words like "integrity," "honor," and "unity." The committee also joined forces with the One Day program to have lunches between the races with a kickoff on July 22, 1999; blacks and whites eating lunch together, getting to know each other.

The committee would evolve, supported by both local and grant monies, to become an important part of the fabric of the city and span small business, the education bureaucracy, and the criminal justice system. The creation of the Mayor's Coalition to Prevent Juvenile Crime in 2004 grew out of the Human Relations Committee as the neighborhood associations began to again experience rising youth crime patterns.

Coming to Florence from Columbia in 2001, new Florence Police Chief Anson Shells saw a spike in juvenile crime, including murders, much of it related to drugs or gangs—so he began to meet with African American church leadership in late 2002 and early 2003. Hearing about the chief's work, Mayor Frank called him to offer his personal and professional services to form a more formal structure, to be supported by the city but also in partnership with other agencies, the faith-based community, the education bureaucracy, and the Florence business community. Chief Shells accepted, and the city supported the new partnership. Several years later, as the organization evolved to include ever more nonprofit organizations, the chief began to call the new effort the "the Mayor's Coalition" (rather than the Mayor's Coalition to Prevent Juvenile Crime) and that name has stuck.

The new Mayor's Coalition developed a mission statement: "To improve the conditions affecting life satisfaction of all citizens in the City of Florence"—which is still carried on coalition literature. Jim Shaw, from Florence 1 Schools, became the first coalition coordinator, later replaced by Chief Shells in 2010, which became full-time work for Shells in 2013 upon his retirement as police chief; his current title in the Florence Police Department is Commander Shells. Dr. Pam Imm, a community psychologist with the University of South Carolina, has provided development services to the coalition; Richard Savage has provided organizational development consulting services, which is his expertise. For its first two years, the coalition was able to fund its startup, organizational costs, and programs with a Federal Grant from the US Department of Juvenile Justice and other funding from Florence 1 Schools. The Youth Services Expo, a major event sponsored by the coalition on Saturday, September 19, 2015, was held at Poynor Adult Education facility, allowing the public and support organizations belonging to the coalition to intermingle, distribute literature, and network; the expo was promoted by Dana Spivey of the Girl Scouts, picking up on the Marion County Impact Festival from the previous year. The primary purpose of the expo was to provide all of Florence information on the cornucopia of beneficial youth-directed services in our area. The South Carolina Department of Juvenile Justice, a key coalition partner, found a home downtown at 181 North Irby St. in the courthouse complex.

The coalition has always been loosely organized with the co-ordinator functioning more as an information and transfer agent and general organizer rather than specifically directing projects. Currently, about 60 organizations are involved, the most prominent being HopeHealth, the City of Florence, Durant Centers, Florence 1 Schools, the School Foundation, the Naomi Project, Pee Dee Community Action Partnership, South Carolina Legal Services, the Housing Authority of Florence, Pee Dee Regional Transportation, Francis Marion University (its FMU Family Support Center), SiMT, Community Crises Response and Intervention, House of Hope, Pee Dee Mental Health, the Salvation Army, Circle Park, Mercy Medical Free Clinic, SC Thrive, and others. The coalition gets both routine communications from Commander Shells and emergent issue communications, often asking for cross-referrals, advice, or practical help among the coalition members. The coalition continues to meet about every other month in the city council chambers for detailed program updates and often featuring speakers; the speakers' programs are diverse, including education, city updates, police updates, SC Voc Rehab, United Way, the Red Cross, mental health, and others. The meetings provide further opportunity for networking across the coalition.

Over time, the new coalition absorbed more and more of what the old Mayor's Committee on Human Relations was doing on the ground in the neighborhoods, in particular with the "No One Un-sheltered" program (coordination of homeless shelter programs and facilities across Florence) and the "Family Support Services Center" (which provides comprehensive crisis intervention through intensive case management). The coalition also worked on summer youth programs, establishing four summer youth centers around the city to provide lunches donated by school volunteers and supervised recreation at several churches and city recreation facilities. About one hundred kids each summer got jobs mostly at fast-food restaurants subsidized by the city through the coalition. The proximate result was about a 30 percent reduction in Juvenile crime, intangible goodwill, and a cooperative spirit in and among Florentines. These results have attracted attention, kudos, and several yearly Achievement Awards from the South Carolina Municipal Association.

The coalition letterhead now reads: "The Mayor's Coalition: Full Life. Full Forward. Florence, South Carolina." The body of any letter also carries the mission statement: "To improve the conditions affecting life satisfaction for all citizens in the City of Florence."

Historical and editorial assistance came from Commander Anson Shells, Drew Griffin, Amanda Pope, and George Jebaily, including access to some of the files of Commander Shells, George Jebaily, and the City of Florence.

The Veterans Park

MAYOR FRANK WILLIS always wanted to respect and honor Florence military veterans. Florence was the home of a former Confederate prison camp and cemetery (called the Florence Stockade); after the Civil War, a new National Cemetery was built near the Stockade on donated land along what is now called National Cemetery Road. It has become an important National Shrine and US Veterans Cemetery and is still used for many Veteran events. The Stockade has been preserved with walking trails, a viewing stand, and historical markers. Frank Willis himself donated some land to increase and enhance the National Cemetery. A reception center was built in 2015.

In 1997, Councilman Bill Bradham, then recently elected to the city council, had the idea to establish a military memorial on the opposite side of Florence from the National Cemetery. He called his idea the "Circle of Flags." The city council approved, so city planning manager David Williams and public works director Drew Griffin developed the memorial. It was placed at the end of the I-20 Spur coming into Florence. The dedication was held in 1999 and Bill Bradham led the small gathering in the Pledge of Allegiance to the US flag followed by formal comments by Mayor Willis. The memorial was funded by the city and is maintained by the city with irrigated landscaping. The five military flags are in a circle with the US flag, the South Carolina flag, and the POW/MIA flag also surrounding a US flag in the center. The military flags include the Army, Marine Corps, Navy, Air Force, and Coast Guard. The memorial remains an important entrance to Florence from off I-20.

In early 2002, Frank called Thomas Marschel, the Florence Chamber of Commerce executive, and said, "We need a Veterans Park. It would showcase our support of this region's veterans and act as a magnet to attract folks to the Pee Dee region. You are an Army Veteran and community leader. Can you head this effort?" Tom said, "Yes."

Background work continued for several years until plans were finalized in 2005; the park was dedicated in 2008. Initially, Tom Marschel organized a Veterans Park Committee, with Frank Willis as chair, including Carlton Prigden (Marines, retired), Colonel Rocky Gannon (US Army Reserve, retired), Karen Acosta (US Army), Tom Stanton, Herbert Peoples, Michael Montrose, and Rebecca Kanobeloch. The new committee met for the first time in the spring of 2003. The committee was eventually expanded to include Rick Walden (from the Florence County Veterans Service office), Claudia Brown-Grossman (of Brown Memorials), Clifford Gates (Marines, retired), Bruce Mallick (US Army Special Forces), Colonel Barry Wingard (US Army, retired), Reggie Armstrong (US Army, retired), Donnie Carter (US Army), Councilman Bill Bradham, Ron Chatham (US Navy), David Barr (US Army), Drew Griffin, Harvey Jones, Ray McBride (US Army), Kenneth Merriman, sculptor Alex Palkovich, David Phillips (World War II veteran), Paul Pittman (US Army Special Forces), Carlton Prigden (Marines, retired), Jim Shaw (US Army Special Forces), Tunis C. Selby, John Spellman, John Vinson, David Williams, and Kenneth Barnes. Tom Marschel and Rick Walden co-chaired this larger group. One of the committee's first tasks beyond the details of organizational structure and funding was to take a bus ride around Florence, looking for sites. They thought the Busch recycling site would be good, but eventually ended up with six acres behind the Civic Center, on land generously donated by the Byrd Estate and Representative Ed Young.

The site selection work took several years. Once the land was in hand, the committee selected a design company, SGA Architects of Charleston, and got to work. The architect's plans called for an outdoor amphitheater, areas for meditation, space for monuments recognizing multiple services, and plaques honoring individual veterans.

By 2005, the Veterans Park Committee had architectural plans and a budget of about $2 million; monuments, land, and landscaping would cost another $2 million. The mayor announced the park in November 2005. The City of Florence contracted with the FBI for the construction of the park. The $2 million project cost for the park was funded through the city's hospitality funds; infrastructure and road improvement costs were paid by a lease-purchase loan of $3 million arranged through BB&T Bank. Besides the Central Obelisk and the Wall of Honor, the park also includes an amphitheater, a water wall with pool, a steel wall with the oath of enlistment, and a landscaped circular trellis area; a Wall of Honor winds up a path in the back. The park was designed to allow for future placement of monuments, memorials, and plaques. The committee raised funding for the monuments through private donations and the sale of plaques to be placed on the Wall of Honor.

The Chamber of Commerce had a 501(c)(3) entity called "Pee Dee Visions Foundation" that was used to organize the bookkeeping for the committee and hold donations and gifts and sponsorships. A major fundraising technique was to sell plaques for at least $150 (later $300) to Veterans or their families with verifiable identification of honorable discharge (DD 214) for the Wall of Honor. They also solicited individual donations. This group raised about $200,000 over the project timeline. Eventually, the committee formed its own 501(c)(3) organization.

Brown Memorials did much of the Monument work and helped with the early design work. Brown Memorials is now in the hands of fifth-generation ownership, Bran Oswalt, following his mother (Claudia Brown-Grossman), his uncle (Pat Brown), and his grandfather (Bill Brown). Brown Memorials has been providing quality service to our area for a long time with cemetery memorials and other monuments. For the Central Obelisk and Eagle in Flight sculpture, Brown Memorials and Alex Palkovich won the American

Institute of Commemorative Art first place award in 2009 in the Public/Civic Memorials category.

The featured sculptor, Alex Palkovich, was born in the Carpathian Mountains, now part of Ukraine. He made Florence his home from 1998 until 2015, first as Global MRI Manufacturing Manager for GE Healthcare and then as a full-time sculptor. He retired as International Production Manager for MRI at GE Healthcare in 2008. Alex has won numerous awards for his sculptures, including a British Design Award in 1987 and a People's Choice Award from the National Sculpture Society in 2013. In 2015, Alex and his wife Aggie moved to Israel; Alex returns about twice a year, staying at Home2Suites. His public works of art can be found across the state, with the greatest concentration at Florence Veterans Park. In total, you'll find 20 of Alex's sculptures and busts in Florence County.

The Florence Veterans Park Committee and the City of Florence held the official opening and dedication ceremony for the Florence Veterans Park on Veterans Day, November 11, 2008. Members from various branches of the military, both active and retired, took part in the opening ceremonies through the presentation of the colors, the Pledge of Allegiance, the invocation, and the raising of the individual military branch flags. The moderator was Colonel Barry Wingard with keynote speaker Columbia native Major General Charles F. Bolden Jr. (Marines, retired), who is also a former astronaut who spent more time in space than any other. (An interesting story here: Major General Bolden spent so much time with the crowd after the event that he missed his flight from Florence through Charlotte back to Houston and was driven to Charlotte by Bud Ferillo.) Following Bolden's remarks, Mayor Frank Willis had some remarks, then he and sculptor Alex Palkovich unveiled the park's Central Obelisk featuring the Soaring Eagle in Flight statue. The 30-foot, three-sided obelisk represents the six military services (Army, Marines, Navy, Air Force, Coast Guard, and the Merchant Marines); the eagle has an eight-foot wingspan and remains the centerpiece of the park. Florence Veterans Park Committee co-chairs Rick Walden and Thomas Marschel and Karen Acosta from the Florence Police Department—all three Army veterans—then unveiled the Wall of Honor. Reverend Pete Cooper (Marines), of St. John's Episcopal Church, lead the closing prayer.

Many exhibits have been added to the park. Alex Palkovich has created several other monuments since the dedication, including Home Safe and the 9/11 Memorial. Barry Wingard was able to obtain a piece of the limestone wall of the Pentagon, bombed in the 9/11 attack, for the Florence 9/11 Memorial. Barry actually drove from Florence to the Pentagon to pick up the 370-pound limestone piece, #ES76. Home Safe features a soldier returning to the embrace of his family and touches an important emotional cord. New monuments include a ship's bell donated by the Patriots Point Naval & Maritime Museum from the World War I battleship, the USS South Carolina; an anchor from the USCG cutter Comanche; a Marine monument; a Purple Heart monument; a POW/MIA monument; a World War II memorial monument; a Merchant Marine monument; and a US Army memorial. The World War I memorial from the American Legion's World War I Monument was first erected in 1928 and moved over to the Veterans Park in 2016 with the funding assistance of Brown's Memorials, GE Healthcare, the County of Florence, and the South Carolina National Guard.

Other major donors to the Veterans Park include the City of Florence Recreation and Parks Department, the Drs. Bruce and Lee Foundation, Armstrong Wealth Management Group, ESAB, SOPAKCO, the Wingards, the Jebailys, King Cadillac-Buick, Florence Builders, Henry Swink, Marion Swink, Eddie Collins, Gregory Electric, Nucor, Crown Beverages, South Florence High School ROTC, various local garden clubs, Alex Palkovich, Wendell Jones, Fred DuBard, Adams Outdoor Advertising, Hilliard Lyons, 1720 Burger, PBGA (Blue Cross), Pee Dee Orthopedics, Sellers Port A Jon, DAR, Bacot Chapter, Florence American Legion Post #1, Military Order of the Purple Heart, Rolling Thunder, the Marine Corps League of Florence, US Navy, Florence Veterans Honor Guard, Florence County Library System, Daughters of the American Revolution, Florence County Museum, and WPDE-TV15.

Historical and editorial assistance came from Thomas Marschel, Bill Bradham, and Barry Wingard. Photography is a gift of Austin Gilbert.

Visions 2010

FLORENCE CITY manager Tommy Edwards began thinking about deliberate and thoughtful strategic planning for the City of Florence sometime in 1990. He thought the term "Visions" had a good ring to it. The City of Florence established "Visions 2000" with a formal resolution on March 19, 1992, after about six months of planning and discussion and the important support of Mayor Haigh Porter, Florence Chamber president Michael McCall (from Florence Darlington Technical College), and the Greater Florence Chamber of Commerce president, Doug Everett. Tommy Edwards and a few of these leaders made a trip to Rock Hill in July of 1992. Further work resulted in an organizational meeting in February 1993 and then a general meeting on March 3, 1993.

The Visions 2000 Steering Committee members were appointed jointly by the City of Florence and the Florence Chamber of Commerce. From the city were appointed Fred Samra, James Schofield, Carol Davis, Edith Heyward, Curtis Doughtry, David Barr, James McBratney, Reverend Larry McCutcheon, John Outlaw, and Lawrence Smith; from the Chamber of Commerce were appointed Maurice Dake, Jean Leatherman, Rick Sellers, Bill Meyer, Pete Johnson, Fred DuBard, and Stephen Imbeau. Fred Samra was named chair of the steering committee. Committees were established and chairs assigned: cultural city by Stephen Imbeau, functional city by John Outlaw and Pete Johnson, historic city by Gary Brown and Fred DuBard, human relations by David Barr, education by Jean Leatherman, and transportation by Fred DuBard. The committees each developed a strategic plan that was formally presented to the city council on October 18, 1994.

The committee reports to the council included:

Cultural city: a) creation of an arts commission and b) development of a downtown cultural/arts complex

Functional city: a) encouragement of city-wide beautification through the coordination of public, semi-public, and private efforts, b) development of the Clemson Park property with a use that will benefit all, c) provision of clear, comprehensive regulations for each of the 14 zoning districts, d) rewriting the Sign Ordinance, e) establishment of comprehensive zoning, f) expansion of the City of Florence with annexation, g) consolidation of government services, h) economic development, and i) improvement of Central Business District with a special tax district

Historic city: a) identification and emphasis of the symbolic entrances to Florence, b) creation of a historical commission with authority to establish regulations for the preservation of historically significant buildings in the Florence area, and c) creation of a linear park following the path of Jeffries Creek with amenities such as walking and biking trails, public open spaces, and recreational areas which connect existing parks with each other and with public facilities including Freedom Florence Recreational Complex and the Florence Area Civic Center

Human relations: creation of a human relations commission with members selected from a wide range of racial, religious, and ethnic backgrounds

Transportation: a) support of regional transportation needs, b) Florence Regional Airport, c) establishment of a transportation multi-nodal complex, d) improvement of parking requirements, and e) improvement of landscaping requirements.

A Visions 2010 Steering Committee grew out of Mayor Willis's 1997 meeting with Pam Osborne, Dr. Charles Gould, David Williams,

George Jebaily, and Dr. Lee Vickers. Several years earlier on September 26, 1995, Frank had met with George Jebaily, Lee Vickers, Libby Cooper, and Dr. Charles Gould to start a process toward downtown redevelopment they called "Future Florence." Dr. Gould wrote a summary meeting memo arguing for a steering committee for Downtown Florence Development: a master plan, city council resolutions, a timeline, anchor tenants, and a contract with outside consultants.

The original 1998 Florence Visions 2010 Steering Committee was co-chaired by George Jebaily and Thomas Marschel; members included Starlee Alexander, Carolyn Frate, Mindy Taylor (Iseman), Harvey Senseney, Councilman Billy Williams, Henry Hepburn, Mary Hepburn, George Alley, Jack Dowis, Hal Fuller, Thomas Smith, Andrew Kampiziones, Ginger Owen, Jim Byrd, D. Scott Weber, Fred DuBard, Dr. Charles Gould, Beverly Hazelwood, Starr Ward, Freddie Jolley, T. William DeBerry, Townsend Holt, Judith Kammer, Bill Steiner, David Williams, Jumana Swindler, Joan Bilheimer, Michelle Juback, Audrey Cooke, Former Mayor Haigh Porter, Jimmy Rainwater, Stephen Wukela, Loretta Brown, Thomas Ewart, Fred Samra, Denise Richbourg-Fitz, Douglas Hawkins, Dr. Fred Carter, Dr. Joe Nelson, Ron Chatham, Mike Eades, Mayor Frank Willis, Kevin George, Ken Jackson, Linda Johnson, Gerry Madison, Bradley Callicott, Reverend Norman Gamble, and Reynolds Williams.

Ben Boozer of the South Carolina Downtown Development Association (SCDDA) was brought in through the Municipal Association to lead several town hall meetings called Visioning Workshops on January 30 and March 15, 2000. At least three hundred citizens attended these meetings and provided public input and responded to questionnaires. A presentation was made on August 21, 2001, by HDR to present their findings and plan to the committee.

HDR was founded in 1917 and is headquartered in Omaha, Nebraska, with a Charlotte, North Carolina, office (actually, they have 250 offices around the world); they started with water and power plants and continue to develop (mostly large-scale) community projects. HDR started to work with the city even before Visions 2010 was formal. Actually, between 1995 and 2004 Florence worked with several consultants producing several reports, for complicated reasons, but mostly trying to find a fit for Florence that was not too costly. The

SCDDA stayed involved with the Florence work, signing a contract with the successor, the Florence Downtown Development Corporation (FDDC), to work on what they called the Main Street Concept.

The town hall meetings have an interesting story. Pamplico native Dr. John Keith was just starting in his new pediatrics practice with the Eastern Carolina Pediatrics group, having joined them in 1999, and heard about the meetings from his mother, and so came, sitting in the back row. What he heard convinced him that Florence was serious about its future and that he should stay, build his life in Florence, and, when able, begin to invest in Florence. He told George Jebaily that he was going to do exactly that. Dr. Keith graduated from Hanna Pamplico High School in 1986, then Howard University and Howard University Medical School; he finished his residency in pediatric medicine at Duke University Hospital. Dr. Keith is now a successful pediatrician and entrepreneur, buying up downtown real estate and holding ownership in The Library and Dolce Vita restaurants. He owns all the real estate on the east side of that block of North Dargan Street, extending north beyond the new police substation; in fact, the substation, developed in 2008, was his first project, and he is very proud of it. He calls himself Coffea Enterprises from his love for coffee; in fact, he went to Seattle to study coffee roasting.

The move of Florence Darlington Technical College (FDTC) downtown with the Health Science Center in 2001 was a major boost to downtown. The new center was important in changing attitudes about downtown, its safety, and its potential.

A major report was made to the city council on January 14, 2002, by George Jebaily and Thomas Marschel from the Visions 2010 Steering Committee; they described committee work done over the previous two years focusing on downtown development and neighborhood development. A downtown development coordinator, Roy Adams, had already been hired by the City of Florence. Their major proposals were to continue work with HDR, maintain staff, and replace the Visions 2010 Steering Committee with a formal, legally organized Florence Downtown Development Corporation (FDDC).

The new corporation would have a board of 21 members, with the mayor, the Chamber of Commerce president, FMU president, and FDTC president as ex officio members. They also suggested regulatory authority for any necessary statutory or legal changes to move the project forward. The city thus developed a department of urban planning, hiring Phillip Lookadoo, the former coordinator, who replaced Roy Adams when he died of an apparent heart attack on November 10, 2005. Roy Adams was fond of saying "Downtown development is not about black nor white; it's about green, that is ... economic development."

The FDDC was formally organized on June 13, 2002. Its first board was appointed by the city and the Visions 2010 Steering Committee. From the city: Councilman Billy Williams, Starr Ward, Erwin Paxton, Fred Samra, Tom Ewart, Yolanda Melvin, and Randolph Hunter; from the Visions 2010 Steering Committee: Starlee Alexander, William DeBerry, Beverly Hazelwood, Mindy Taylor, George Jebaily, and Jimmy Rainwater. George Jebaily was the first chair. Ex officio members included Dr. Fred Carter, Dr. Charles Gould, Tom Marschel, David Williams, Frank Willis, and Steve Powers.

Concurrent with downtown redevelopment, Visions 2010 and HDR Consulting also provided a guide to neighborhood development and improvement to include two phases. Phase I should include: 1) reconnaissance and inventory, 2) summary analysis plans, 3) concept development, 4) work sessions and community meetings, 5) draft plans and report, 6) community meeting, and 7) final plan. Phase II should include: 1) orientation maps, 2) summary analysis, 3) master plan alternatives, 4) summary of community meetings, 5) draft master plan, and 6) final master plan.

The resulting downtown and master plan was presented to the city council in 2009, finally approved in 2011, and called the Florence Comprehensive Plan; it is now housed as a large document on the city web page, including items both in downtown and in the neighborhoods. You can find the entire document at *cityofflorence.com/city-plans*.

Visions 2010 Steering Committee goals:

Develop a master plan for the downtown that includes a three-dimensional scale model

Advocate location of a Cultural Campus downtown to serve as a focal point of the revitalization of Downtown Florence

Maximize use and appearance of city-owned property and public
   areas

Advocate development of a plan burying utility lines and removing
   billboards

Begin efforts to encourage building renovation

Work to make downtown clean and safe

Develop public education programs to create a more positive attitude
   about downtown

Establish an independent downtown development corporation with
   professional staff as an organizational vehicle for implementing
   the plan

Historical and editorial assistance came from Thomas Marschel, George Jebaily (his
files, too), Dr. John Keith, and Drew Griffin.

Florence County Legislative Day

IN EARLY 2002, Frank Willis, Russ Froneberger, and Dr. Stephen Imbeau were having dinner together at PA's Restaurant in Florence. Russ turned to Steve and asked about legislative contacts; thinking he meant personally, Steve talked about his trips to Columbia to receptions, personal relationships with legislators, and his work with the South Carolina Medical Association. But Russ said, "No, no; I mean your town, your area: do you all have any organized legislative activity in Columbia?" The answer was "no" and Frank and Steve looked at each other. And so, Steve asked what Russ suggested. He said, "You need a yearly legislative reception in Columbia like the big cities." Steve said, "I will call you."

Well, Russ had just consulted with the Spartanburg and Greenville communities to organize such a Columbia legislative event whose first theme was the auto industry, with a new BMW sportster on-site at a Columbia event. He gave Steve the cost data, information about what groups did the organizational work, and so on. Steve called some of the Chamber of Commerce and Development folks in Spartanburg and they were solidly behind the value of the event. As the new chair of the Florence County Development Authority, Dr. Gould liked the idea and viewed a Legislative Day as important.

Dr. Fred Carter from FMU noted the importance other communities attached to their own Legislative Day.

Senator Leatherman's office was solicited for help and the senator took on the project as if it were his own. Robby Dawkins, the political director in the senator's office and a Florence native, sent us a list of the communities sponsoring such events, their style or theme, and whether Robby thought them to be successful or not. Robby also suggested venues around Columbia, and Dr. Gould and Steve Imbeau visited several together; Dr. Gould also visited some sites on his own. The clear pick was the Columbia City Art Museum on Main Street because of its space, kitchen support, available parking, and reasonable pricing.

The project was a natural fit for the City of Florence, the County of Florence, and the Greater Florence Chamber of Commerce. Mindy Taylor (Iseman) and Pete Mazzaroni came on board to staff and organize the first event; they both had organizational success with Carolina Power & Light and Roche Carolina, and both had previously worked with Mayor Frank on other projects.

Osbornes was picked to cater the event, a great decision. To this day, Florence County Legislative Day in Columbia is ranked as having the best food among similar Columbia legislative receptions; and it turns out that food is a very important part of legislative events. Amazingly, Osbornes could put on such a great party with four hundred guests for only $7,000.

Mindy and Pete began small group meetings at Osbornes upstairs lounge. The objectives were: 1) promote Florence to the legislature, 2) educate our business community on the legislative process, and 3) develop leadership in Florence.

Mindy and Pete then set up a Legislative Day Committee that usually met at the Carolina Power & Light/Progress Energy offices, and sometimes at the Chamber of Commerce offices. The members were Mindy and Pete as co-chairs, Gary Brown, Peggy Bowers, Libby Cooper, Mack Davenport, Joan McLeod, Mike Singletary, Dianne Hughes, Robby Dawkins, Tom Marschel, Marshall Yarborough, Sandy Durant, Joan McLeod, and Miriam Swiler. Florence County Legislative Day was born.

The first reception had to be special to continue on, to make a "statement." The committee worked very hard, and Senator Leatherman and his staff worked just as hard. The funding was agreed to be $10,000 each from the City of Florence (Frank and city manager David Williams), the County of Florence (chair Rusty Smith and manager Joe King), and Florence County Progress (chair George Wilds and director Mike Eades). The first date was set for March 11, 2003, and Robby Dawkins made sure it was on the legislative calendar a year in advance.

The theme of the first reception was "Passport to Florence: Unlocking the Potential of the Pee Dee." Corporate participants included Carolina Hospitals System, the City of Florence, the County of Florence, Florence County Economic Development Partnership, FDTC, FMU, Honda Manufacturing of South Carolina, IRIX Pharmaceuticals, Maytag, McLeod Regional Medical Center, Nan Ya Plastics, Pee Dee Touchstone Commerce City, Progress Energy, Science South, and Roche Carolina. Senator Leatherman was the featured speaker. Tom Marschel and Kerry Floyd, who had done training films for Sonoco, developed an important promotional video on Florence to use at the reception. The video was an important part of this first event. Entertainment was provided by Savannah Grove Baptist Church, The Forenzi Strings, and The Woodys.

Passports to the reception were sent to each legislator, and gifts (very nice CD boxes) were hand-delivered to each legislator's Columbia office a week or so ahead of the event. Senator Leatherman called the Senate members and put a flier on each Senate seat the day before the event. The turnout was excellent. Senator Vern Smith, the oldest person in the South Carolina Senate, told all attending that it was the best local community reception he had ever been to and wanted to make sure Florence came back the next year.

About 50 Florentines came for the day of the first reception and were given lunch, followed by a tour conducted by Robby Dawkins of the State House, the Capitol Dome, the Governor's and Lieutenant Governor's offices, and Senator Leatherman's Senate Finance Committee hearing room. Senator Leatherman led the tour in the Gressette Senate Office Building and his demonstration of the hearing room. Attorney General McMaster met with the group briefly as well. Folks went over to relax and change clothes at the South Carolina Beer Association offices before the evening reception.

Starting in 2004, the programs became more formal, and the luncheons were supported by several Florence-area Banks. The motif for the 2004 reception was luggage tags with the theme of "The Florence County Connection." In 2004, the lunch agenda included presentations by Lieutenant Governor Andre Bauer, Senator Hugh Leatherman, President pro tempore Glenn McConnell, Speaker David Wilkins, and Mayor Willis. The afternoon program was in a lecture hall and included Governor Mark Sanford, Secretary of Commerce Bob Faith, Chad Prosser (director of parks), and President of the State Chamber Hunter Howard. The evening reception visitors were greeted in the Columbia Art Museum Plaza by two Pee Dee Pride Hockey players in full uniform.

Senator Kent Williams was the luncheon speaker in 2005, and the afternoon program that year included presentations by the governor, the director of parks, and Bill Steiner, the Directory of Community Builders. The governor also hosted a tour of the Mansion. Josh Turner was the entertainment.

The legislative gifts were a nice CD box (2003), luggage tags (2004), and a telescope (2005). The event was turned over to the Florence County Economic Development Partnership office for the 2006 event and it has been managed from there ever since with Joe King as director. The organizing committee continues, with normal turnover of volunteer members. The yearly legislative gifts continue and remain popular. The Partnership now gives the legislative staff a very nice ink pen each year with the inscription "Florence County Legislative Day." Robby Dawkins told us he heard positive comments about the pens at least once a month, all year long. The Partnership now awards door prizes donated by the event's corporate advertisers, and the door prizes have also proved very popular. Quentin Hawkins is now Senator Leatherman's liaison.

As of 2020, the Florence County Legislative Day has been hosted 19 times.

Historical and editorial assistance came from Senator Hugh Leatherman, Dr. Charles Gould, Robby Dawkins, Mindy Taylor, Pete Mazzaroni (including their committee meeting minutes), and Joe King.

YEAR	BUDGET	ATTENDANCE	GIFT
2006	$30,000	300	Map portfolio
2007	$30,000	300	Jane Jackson print, Florence
2008	$30,000	300	Globe puzzle
2009	$30,000	300	Balance scale and book weights
2010	$30,000	300	Compass with box
2011	$30,000	350	Letter opener
2012	$30,000	350	Magnifying glass
2013	$30,000	350	Leather mouse pad
2014	$30,000	425	Journal notebook
2015	$30,000	500	Ceramic stone coasters
2016	$30,000	300	Bamboo cutting boards
2017	$30,000	300	Black wine leather carriers
2018	$30,000	500	Backpacks, Florence County
2019	$30,000	300	Carolina wren candles
2020	$30,000	300	Florence County Museum stationary
2021		Virtual (COVID-19)	Pecan and cheese straws, Young Pecan

All gifts are inscribed with the year, "Florence County Legislative Day" and the county seal.

SiMT

THE SOUTHEASTERN Institute of Manufacturing and Technology (SiMT) was the brainchild of Dr. Charles Gould as he studied technical school education around the world and looked to expand and enrich the experience at FDTC in Florence. His basic idea was to have a center with advanced manufacturing and computer technology that could assist commercial and government industries in employee job training as well as prototype development and advanced technology training. This would also provide education opportunities for FDTC students in the same institute. Corporate employees would come into the institute for discrete blocks of training, staying at local hotels or apartments, with contract support from the employer to FDTC. Someday, the institute could also become a business project incubator.

After long thought and study, including some modeling and promotion work in 2002, Dr. Gould began serious work on the project.

The college did most of the work internally with some outside consulting. Dr. Gould broke the effort into several phases: 1) develop the idea, 2) sell the idea to Florence, FDTC's leadership, and then solicit input, 3) design and build the facilities, and 4) implement. Most of the work was done under Dr. Gould's direction, with a team at FDTC including Morrison Keaster, Jack Roach, Ed Bethea, and Charlie Muse. Board and foundation members Goz Segars and

Fred DuBard were also heavily involved in the development and implementation of the concept. Other members of the FDTC board at that time included Willie Boyd Sr., Alvin DeWitt, R. Bryan Harwell, Annie Jett, Mary Langston, Allan McLeland, J. Erwin Paxton, and Thomas Perrin; the Foundation Board included Fred DuBard, Joan Bilheimer, Mark Buyck III, Hugh Campbell, Brian Caperton, Lee Crawford, James Griggs, EJ Newby, Tom Kinard, Cindy Griggs, Bill Johnson, James Odom, Howard Peterson, Jim Ramsey, Frank Willis, and Guy Steenrod. Dr. Gould was the FDTC president.

The final vision for the project was presented by Dr. Gould himself in an essay:

> "Florence Darlington Technical College (FDTC) has been serving the Pee dee are residents for nearly 42 years. FTDC's tradition of offering quality education programs that support economic development and the dreams and aspirations of our customers has fueled the College's recent phenomenal growth spurt. In fact, FDTC ranked as the faster growing instruction of higher education in South Carolina during the 1995-1999 period (Higher Education Statistical Abstract '99, page 3).
>
> Total headcount enrollment in the College's curriculum programs now stand at nearly 4,000 students. FDTC's Continuing Education Division has also experience rapid growth (often more that 30 percent per year) in recent years and served more than 30,000 customers during the last calendar year.
>
> Much of FDTC's growth has been driven by economic development in Florence and Darlington Counties. Rocher Carolina, Inc, NanYa Plastic, and Honda of South Carolina - to mention a few of the more recognizable names—have chosen to locate facilities in the heart of South Carolina's Pee Dee region. In fact, Florence County has enjoyed nearly $1 billion in economic investment in the past five years. Darlington County has seen more than $550 million during the same period.
>
> Changes in technology at existing industries, new technologies at relocating industry, and shrinking state appropriations (exacerbated by the recent economic downturn), however, are making it more and more difficult for FDTC to serve the advanced technological needs of the area's manufacturing industries. If the current brisk pace of economic development is to be sustained in the coming decade, it is imperative

that FDTC be positioned to meet tomorrows' educational and economic development challenges.

To remain among the leaders of technical education in South Carolina, FDTC must seek answers to a host of factors that are converging to shape the future of education and the economic health of our region. Creating a learning centered environment (as opposed to a teacher-centered environment); producing skilled workers; keeping pace with technology; supporting existing industries; accom-modulating a non-traditional student; establishing a secure revenue stream; and being proactive in economic development activities are challenges that FDTC must be prepared to meet.

This publication's purpose is to explain FDTC's answers to tomorrow's challenges. It will show how FDTC is planning to use a recently acquired 146-acre tract of land behind the main campus to establish a technology park comprised of eight highly focused technical institutes—each of which will focus on a specific area of technology and on an economic development trend. Once established, some of these institutes will be revenue generators and will provide state-of-the-art training in tomorrow's technology.

The global marketplace has made it imperative that FDTC take a proactive stand in preparing for tomorrow's education needs. At FDTC we are excited about the possibilities that the future holds, and we invite you to review this publication and see our plans for making FDTC an avenue to technical excellence. Charles W Gould, FDTC President"

A series of meetings was held in the Osbornes entrance hall with many community leaders for presentation and feedback; leaders giving active support included Mike Eades, Emerson Gower, Jim Ramsey, Ray Harris, Ron Rogers, Frank Jones, Fred DuBard, Robert Williams, Don Herriott, Mayor Frank Willis, and Moot Truluck. A final report to the community was presented at Osbornes on December 3, 2003. In addition, site visits were made by college staff and board members to several schools around the United States looking at both similar institutes and some of those with the proposed computer technology, including trips to Cleveland, Ohio, Racine, Wisconsin, and San Diego, California. Many of the trips were funded through the generosity of Powers Aviation and Billy Powers.

The project was broken into phases, of which Phase I and Phase II are complete. Phase I includes the Advanced Manufacturing Center, the Additive Manufacturing Center, the 3D Virtual Reality Center, and the National Robotics Training Center. The cost of Phase I was about $37 million, with about $25 million paid under FDTC's own bonding authority. Senator Hugh Leatherman helped obtain the original land and some South Carolina State Funding—the Phase I facility, the Advanced Manufacturing Center, is named for him. Groundbreaking for Phase I was held on October 4, 2004, and the grand opening was held on September 26, 2007. The construction was completed by Choate Construction Company.

Phase II included the Manufacturing and Business Incubator and was funded internally for about $6 million and opened in 2014. Administrators of the Phase I facility included Mark Roth, Tressa Gardner, David McBride, and currently Mark Roth, while the Phase II facility was first managed by Ashley Dingle and now Patricia Gardner.

The use of the facility has been enthusiastic with contracts from Honda, GE, GM, Caterpillar, BMW, Boeing, the US Navy, and the US Army. FDTC students are most enthusiastic about it. The center has also provided important meeting facilities for both local and national clients with its own auditorium, catering kitchens, and meeting and exhibit halls.

Historical and editorial assistance came from Dr. Charles Gould, Ed Bethea, and Jill Lewis. Dr. Gould wrote much of this chapter.

NESA

THE NORTH Eastern Strategic Alliance (NESA) was conceived and born in Florence at the FMU offices of Dr. Fred Carter, president of the university. Several concept meetings in the early fall of 2000 with Billy Alford, Ron Ingle, Yancey McGill, Frank Willis, Fred DuBard, Senator Leatherman, Doug Wendel, Mark Kelly, and Tom Keegan lead to an organizational meeting in later fall. The concept was to develop regional cooperation for economic development based on the strengths of Myrtle Beach and Florence. Ron Ingle and Dr. Fred Carter were the first co-chairs.

NESA was incorporated on January 29, 2001, and several of the above members formed the core executive committee. Members Carter, McGill, and Leatherman continue to the present (as of 2020). The original NESA Board included Senator Yancey McGill, Senator Hugh Leatherman, Representative Doug Jennings, Representative Mark Kelley, Mayor Frank Willis, Dr. Fred Carter, Dr. Ron Ingle, Fred DuBard, and Doug Wendell. The NESA office was first located on the Campus of Coastal Carolina University and then moved to 121 South Evander Dr. #114 and is now at 142 North Dargan St. (University Place).

Mayor Frank had long believed in regional cooperation, particularly for utilities and economic development. As mayor, he worked with Florence, Darlington, Marion, and Marlboro counties on water and sewer and obtained good results with several, providing service to Darlington and Marion. Frank worked with Robert Williams on the regional airport concept. Frank worked with the State of South Carolina Department of Commerce on fostering regional economic development cooperation and cluster services/industry development. Several years earlier he also put together a group to initiate what they called the Pee Dee Economic Development Partnership, starting with the counties of Florence, Darlington, Dillon, and Marion, but that effort was put aside in favor of NESA.

The NESA mission statement was straightforward: "NESA's mission is to work with existing county and state economic development organizations to create new jobs and increase the per capita wage of the citizens of the North Eastern region of South Carolina at a rate faster than the per capita growth rates for the state and the nation." The counties involved include Chesterfield, Darlington, Dillon, Florence, Georgetown, Horry, Marion, Marlboro, and Williamsburg. Ron Chatham was the first executive director. Yancey McGill became the first chair on October 30, 2002. Jeff McKay was hired to succeed Ron Chatham on December 4, 2005. He continues to this day.

Jeff McKay graduated from Western Carolina University undergraduate and graduate school and is certified as an economic developer by the International Economic Development Council. He worked first in several North Carolina counties and then for the State of North Carolina Department of Commerce. He came to Florence directly from the Greater Statesville Development Corporation.

The NESA organizers were also clever to attract private support to expand its funding and thus its clout and reach. Along the way, many businesses have been involved, including Duke Energy, FTC and HTC, Blue Cross, Santee Cooper, Anderson Brothers Bank, Sonoco, Honda, Pee Dee Electric, Horry Electric Cooperative, Marlboro Electric Cooperative, Arbor One, AT&T, the Brandon Agency, Burroughs and Chapin, Nucor, Pepsi, SC Bank and Trust, the Yahnis Corporation, South Carolina Port Authority, SCANA, TD Bank, South Carolina Power, MB Kahn, the Jackson Companies, Grand Strand Water, the Myrtle Beach Chamber of Commerce, Wells Fargo, PGBA, Cyberwoven, DSM, Roche Carolina, Sandhills Telephone, Sun

Construction, Alliance Engineers, BNC, Carlisle Associates, Nexsen Pruet, SME, Thomas Hutton, Darlington Raceway, Dominion Energy, MEC, Truist, Wells Fargo, AECOM, S+ME, and Fitts Godwin.

From the NESA web page (*nesasc.org*):

The NESA staff has the resources and expertise to assist companies interested in relocating or expanding in the region. Our customized service insures that you have access to all of the components needed to jump-start *your* business including:

Regional site selection—NESA will work with representatives from each of its nine counties to identify the best buildings or sites based on your company's needs. From there, extensive research and guided site tours allow you to make a fully educated decision before you commit.

Regional demographic and socioeconomic data—NESA has access to numerous databases and research resources that it will use to provide up-to-date information that will help your company make an informed decision about locating a facility in the region.

Infrastructure—NESA will work with CSX (railroad), the South Carolina Department of Transportation, water and sewer authorities, telecommunications companies, and energy companies to identify locations that have the infrastructure your company requires to be successful.

Coordination with State and Local Permitting Entities and Utilities

Facilitation of community briefings, custom tours, and building or site tours

Incentives—NESA will coordinate with its county allies and the South Carolina Department of Commerce to develop competitive incentives packages, making locating in the NESA Region one of the easiest and best business decisions you have ever made.

Workforce—Through resources offered by the Southeastern Institute of Manufacturing and Technology (SiMT) and ReadySC, the NESA Region has the resources to provide you with a world-class workforce that will ensure your profitability and success in the region for years to come.

Services to County Allies

NESA's core services to its county members include:

Product Development—NESA supports its counties through product development assistance and initiatives.

Research—NESA maintains up-to-date information that can be used for RFI's and will also assist each county with preparing these documents for companies and consultants. In addition, NESA subscribes to a proprietary database of nearly 14 million companies worldwide and will use this database to assist county allies in their lead generation and research efforts.

Marketing—NESA markets the region locally, domestically, and internationally and provides its services to each county economic development group for specific marketing projects.

Business Development—NESA encourages its local economic developers to participate in its domestic and international business development missions. These missions are organized, planned, and executed by NESA.

Current board members include Yancey McGill (chair), Dr. Fred Carter, Senator Luke Rankin, Senator Hugh Leatherman, Dr. Michael Benson, Buddy Brand, Senator Kent Williams, Former Mayor Stephen Wukela, Representative Roger Kirby, Mark Lazarus, Mary Anderson, Stuart Ames, John Atkinson, Benjy Hardee, Dr. Linda Hayes, Angela Christian, Senator Gerald Malloy, Dr. Tiffany Wright, John Bloom, Jason Steen, and Johnny Gardner. Current staff includes Jeff McKay (executive director), Andrew Golden, John Sweeney, Amber Sellers, Jeffrey DeLung, and Rich Spivery. It is important to note that only 4 percent of NESA funds and revenues are used for basic staffing; 5 percent is used for its supporters, an impressive 17 percent for marketing (but this also includes some staff costs), and an all-important 24 percent for business development. NESA funding for 2014 was $2.27 million and by 2020 had grown to $2.4 million.

The results have been impressive. Jobs created through direct NESA contacts were 978 for 2007, 2,689 for 2008, 965 for 2009, 1,356 for 2010, 2,151 for 2011, 1,477 for 2012, 1,477 for 2012, 2,229 for 2013 and 1,633 for 2014. Resulting capital investments include $216 million in 2007, $253 million in 2008, $411 million in 2009, $129 million in 2010, $249 million in 2011, $326 million in 2012, $247 million in 2013 and $355 million in 2014. There were 14 substantial announcements in 2014 with about 95 leads pursued, resulting in a growth of 1,700 net jobs. In 2019, the dollar totals of business done are also impressive: real estate was $1.5 million, warehouse and transport were $31.8 million, retail was $3.3 million, and professional and scientific was $1.8 million.

The 3,400-acre Inland Port Dillon was finished in 2018 and has been very important for the NESA region (taken directly from the NESA web page):

> Inland Port Dillon is the latest gem in the South Carolina Ports Authority's extensive infrastructure. Located in the NESA region on I-95 and 30 minutes from the eastern origin of I-20, Inland Port Dillon is the answer to your supply chain needs. Dillon enjoys quality direct rail service via CSX's Class 1 railway and is serviced by nearly a dozen ocean carriers. Nestled in a 3,400-acre industrial park that includes available speculative buildings—and in a region boasting over 100 industrial sites with an average price of $17,000 per acre and more than 30 available buildings—Inland Port Dillon can give you the advantage you've been looking for.

For obvious reasons, NESA staff work hard to develop relationships with site consultants wherever they can find them. NESA is a success story for our region and a model of regional cooperation for South Carolina.

Historical and editorial assistance came from Dr. Fred Carter and Jeff McKay, as well as some of the writing. Final review by Jeff McKay.

Infrastructure: Water and Sewer

FRANK ALSO had a vision for water and sewer expansion not only to better serve the city, but also FDTC, FMU, and the surrounding communities. Water supplies are provided through a system of groundwater treatment, surface water treatment, and wastewater treatment systems acting in balance to respond to demand and supply. All have been upgraded since 1995 with new surface water facilities at the Pee Dee Electric Industrial Park, upgrades at the wastewater facility on Stockade Road, and new wells and towers. Although lowly and out of the way, the new facilities are very important in the development of all of Florence, including the downtown. Frank worked with Robert Williams, Tom Kinard, and others to build the new surface water treatment plant in the Pee Dee Touchstone Energy City Industrial Park to reclaim Pee Dee River water; the project was aptly named the Pee Dee Rivers Project. The new plant was finished in 2002 and the Stockade Road facility upgraded in 2012, with room for expansion. In addition, the city took over the County of Florence water and sewer system at least to the Lynches River by agreement dated May 23, 2002, implementing by staff in 2003, providing important expansion, efficiencies, and revenue. The Florence system now has a capacity of more than 40 million gallons per day, plenty of clean water for Florence's expansion. But to provide even more capacity for growth potential, another facility is the planning stages.

Financing for all this was loosely called the Pee Dee Rivers Initiative (formally the Florence Pee Dee Water and Sewer Committee)—loosely because the Initiative also included work with Carolina Power & Light, Alcoa, and the town of Georgetown. The water for the Pee Dee River system water usage and related projects mostly originates in the Yakin River system and dammed lakes in North Carolina and is managed by the City of Florence Finance Department, particularly Thomas Chandler. Starting in 1999, or even earlier, the city applied for and obtained a series of special loans, bonding, and grants for the water and sewer system expansion and upgrade expense. These included a state revolving fund loan of $2,767,997 (1999); a 30-year bond for $25,690,000 at the same time obtaining a Moody's Bond Rating upgrade from A2 to A1 (2000); a state revolving fund loan of $6,210,343 (2000); a State of South Carolina Infrastructure revolving fund loan of $4,062,403; revenue bonds of $8,360,000 to finance the takeover of the County of Florence system (2002); state revolving loan fund of $2,517,834 (2003); revenue bonds of $2 million—specifically for expansion to Windsor Forest, Grove Park, Lakewood, Forest Lake Shores, the Meadows and Womack Gardens, and two associated new pump stations (2003); rebate of about $123,000 of certain sales taxes previously paid to both local energy companies; and stormwater revenue bonds of $4 million (2006). While $50 million is a lot of money, without it, the city and even the county would have limited growth potential and limited business recruitment. Along the way, utility rates were adjusted to account for the growth and debt by city resolution in 2007; even so, Florence utility rates remain very competitive with the rest of the state. (All the data in this paragraph was extracted from the "Thomas Chandler Memo" of 2018, provided by the City of Florence.)

The South Carolina Drought of 1999–2000 prompted keen interest in water and sewer projects, in addition to the need for water to enable economic development. Water is one of those commodities we think we have plenty of . . . until we don't. Most of us don't think about water at all; but water plays an important role in tourism and recreation, energy production, wastewater treatment, drinking water, agriculture, parks, lawns, and gardens. Fresh water flow also keeps salt water out of our rivers. The drought reduced flows in the Pee Dee River-Yadkin River basin endangering citizens from Cheraw to Georgetown and Myrtle Beach; at one point in its course, the Pee Dee River fell to about three feet compared to its normal 20 feet. Mayor Frank along with a core group of seven folks (chair Robert Grooms, Ronnie Ward, Eibert Warren, Henry Peoples, Ray Harris, Gene Butler, and Frank Jones) organized the Florence Pee Dee Regional Water and Sewer Steering Committee, adding 32 regular members to meet about once a month from 2000 to 2005, managed by David Brown of Davis and Brown Engineers. Chairman Robert Grooms was the mayor of Lamar, a school principal, and one of those politicians who know everybody and is fearless in making contacts and arranging for grant monies.

The committee led to action in regional water and sewer cooperation, discussions with Carolina Power & Light, improved liaison with the South Carolina Department of Health and Environmental Control and the State of North Carolina, and the significant improvement in the City of Florence surface water treatment capacity noted above. Freddy Vang, deputy director of the South Carolina Department of Natural Resources, along with the steering committee, worked with North Carolina, the power companies, and the Federal Energy Regulatory Commission to increase flow from CPL lakes in North Carolina feeding the Yadkin system, but without much success; the Florence and South Carolina folks were hoping for a shared water formula with the North Carolina folks. Rainfall solved most problems, but the foundation was once again laid for regional cooperation.

The Yadkin-Pee Dee Rivers Basin is dotted with important power plants on the following lakes: W. Kerr Scott Reservoir, High Rock Lake, Tuckertown Reservoir, Badin Lake, Falls Reservoir, Lake Tillery, and Blewitt Falls Lake.

From Wikipedia:

All but W. Kerr Scott generate hydroelectric power. High Rock, Tuckertown, Badin, and Falls Reservoir were managed by Alcoa under contract with the US Government, under oversight by the Federal

Energy Regulatory Commission (FERC). The contract with FERC expired in April 2008 and was under review after the N.C. Division of Water Quality revoked their water-quality certificate that the company needs to continue operating its power-generating dams along the river. The governor of North Carolina, Bev Perdue, and other North Carolina politicians made it a priority to recapture the Yadkin River water rights, but this has been denied. On September 22, 2016, Alcoa received a license to operate until March 31, 2055, a period 12 years shorter than desired. The license requires a minimum water level and a swimming beach for High Rock Lake. The terms of the license will now apply to Cube Hydro Carolinas, which bought the hydroelectric power operations.

Lake Tillery and Blewitt Falls Lake were managed by Carolina Power & Light. North Carolina and South Carolina have yet to agree on a water sharing formula.

Infrastructure:
Downtown Florence

DOWNTOWN FLORENCE was developed for the first time from about 1890 to 1920 with some of the magnificent buildings that still grace our city. In fact, about 30 of these buildings were placed on the National Register for Historic Buildings in 2008.

The streets were first laid out in 1854 to include Evans, Dargan, Cheves, Coit, and Irby, mostly named after prominent families or businesses of the time. Although occasionally disturbed by fire, major development began in about 1890 by the business families of the time, including the Aikens, Sanborns, Zeiglers, Waterses, Nofals, Kukers, and Kresses. Many of their descendants live in Florence today, and some of their businesses even survive.

Some of the buildings or businesses had interesting names, such as "Hat Box," "Blue Bird Tea Room," "Oscars Salon," "Boinest Hardware," and the "Rose Building." Now we are witness to a rebirth of these buildings as our downtown undergoes an awakening.

During the time of Mayor David McLeod, federal funding paid for some urban redevelopment that basically resulted in some buildings that were beyond repair being torn down and some new living units built outside the downtown. But there was really very little redevelopment of our downtown.

During the time of Mayor Cooper Tedder, the city tried to change

Evans Street with new storefronts, overhead cement awnings, and a new fountain at Harllee Square. The goal was to position downtown to compete with the new malls springing up on the west side of town, but it didn't work.

During the time of Mayor Rocky Pearce, the awnings were taken down and the square became part of the new Business and Technology Center, and modern Florence downtown redevelopment began.

Redevelopment became serious with Mayor Frank.

The city hired its first developer dedicated to downtown, Roy Adams, in 2001; when he died on November 10, 2005, the city hired Philip Lookadoo—who now works in the city planning department. Next was Ray Reich in 2011 and then Hannah Davis in 2019.

At about the same time, the Drs. Bruce and Lee Foundation—formed in 1995 from the purchase profits of the Florence General and Bruce Hospitals—began to provide funding for small public projects using an existing tax-exempt status, with formal IRS designation coming in 2001. Also, the growth spurt of McLeod Hospital afforded a large commercial base for downtown. Florence was poised for growth not seen since the early 1900s.

Frank started to work on downtown development as soon as September 26, 1995, when he met with George Jebaily, Lee Vickers, Libby Cooper, and Dr. Charles Gould to start a process toward downtown redevelopment they called "Future Florence"; after this meeting, Dr. Gould wrote a memo arguing for a steering committee to develop: a master plan, city council resolutions, A timeline, anchor tenants, and contracts with outside consultants. Several committees came and went until the formation of Visions 2010 in 1999. In the next three to five years, a lot was done with the guidance of HDR Engineering, the SCDDA, and Hunter Interests. Hunter Interests, an economic consulting company that was organized in 1986 by Donald Hunter in Annapolis, Maryland, was brought in once the Florence Downton Development Corporation was organized. Hunter Interests provided a series of reports and guideposts in early 2004 and continued work until 2009.

The Florence Downtown Development Corporation (FDDC) was formally organized on June 13, 2002. Its first board was appointed by the city and the Visions 2010 Steering Committee. From the city:

Councilman Billy Williams, Starr Ward, Erwin Paxton, Fred Samra, Tom Ewart, Yolanda Melvin, and Randolph Hunter; from the Visions 2010 Steering Committee: Starlee Alexander, William DeBerry, Beverly Hazelwood, Mindy Taylor, George Jebaily, and Jimmy Rainwater. George Jebaily was the first chair and remains. Ex officio members included Dr. Fred Carter, Dr. Charles Gould, Tom Marschel, David Williams, Frank Willis, and Steve Powers. The first director was Roy Adams. The current board includes Scott Collins, Brian Falcone, Dr. Fred Carter, Starlee Alexander, Ed Love, Carl Humphries, Randy Osterman, Veronica Robertson, Tim Norwood, and Mayor Teresa Myers-Ervin. The director is Hannah Davis.

The Doctors Bruce and Lee Foundation was started with a corpus of about $90 million which has grown to about $250 million despite substantial contributions along the way. The original Foundation Board from 1995 was the combined boards of the former Florence General Hospital and Bruce Hospital System: Dr. Frank B. Lee was the first chair and Bradley Callicott was the first and current director; Dr. Eddie Floyd is the current chair. The Foundation hired Bradley Callicott in August 1995 as director. Other board members in 1995 included Charles Boyd, Ben Dozier, William Tallevast, Elting Chapman, Willis Gregory, Fred Jones, Bobby O'Harra, Johnny Thomason, Dr. John Bruce, Thomas Griffin, Gordon Baker, Mark Buyck Jr., Henry Swink, John McGinnis, and Haigh Porter. The board now is Dr. Eddie Floyd as chair, Mark Buyck Jr., Haigh Porter, Dr. John Bruce, Gordon Baker, Dr. Frank Lee Jr., Dr. Coleman Buckhouse, Henry Swink, Kim Turner, and Allison Tanner.

The mission statement of the Foundation is "To advance the general welfare and quality of life in the Florence area by providing economic support to qualified programs and nonprofits. In furthering its mission, the Foundation pledges to support a broad range of charitable purposes including medical, health, human services, education, arts, religion, civic affairs, as well as the preservation and promotion of cultural, historical, and environmental resources." The Foundation established a set of guidelines: grants will be limited to projects and programs that specifically impact the Florence, South Carolina area; grants will be limited to duly established organizations that have been granted charitable status per section 501(c)

(3) of the Internal Revenue Code or units of government; grants for specific projects and or equipment will be emphasized, as opposed to the funding of the operating expenses; the Foundation does not purchase tickets for or otherwise participate in fundraising events; challenge or matching grants will be considered whenever possible; grants to individuals will not be considered; applications must demonstrate the financial potential to sustain the program or project after Foundation funding is exhausted; multi-year grants, not to exceed three years, may be considered; proposed projects and programs must be consistent with the Foundation's mission statement, charitable purpose, and its current grants focus.

The move of Florence Darlington Technical College to Downtown Florence with the Health Science Center in 2001 was a major early boost to downtown. The Drs. Bruce and Lee Foundation helped the move with a $920,000 grant, its first major downtown donation. The new center was important in changing attitudes about downtown, its safety, and its potential.

The City of Florence's early adoption of the new Hospitality Tax (newly enacted by the State Legislature in 1997) was very important, providing up to 2 percent of property taxes from hospitality, mostly motels, hotels, and restaurants in the city limits with infrastructure funding. The Hospitality Tax provided about $2 million additional in its first year. In addition, the downtown landlords were amenable to a special Tax Incentive Financing District (TIF) for the downtown area. Working with the city manager, the planning and urban development department, the public works department, and the city's bond attorneys, a TIF was established for Downtown Florence by the city council on December 18, 2006, implemented in 2007. In addition, the city successfully competed for a 10-year low-interest loan of $300,000 from the US Economic Development Loan and Grant Program in September of 2007; this money was used for green space, parking, and pedestrian pathways in downtown Florence. Councilman Ed Robinson and George Jebaily worked hard to bring both the downtown and periphery merchants and landowners into accepting these measures with literature handouts and face-to-face visits.

Designated Phase I, the initial planning work for a new downtown was accomplished between 1995 and 2004 and, after several studies, set up the following major goals in a report from Hunter Interests on August 17, 2004:

- National Register district must be considered as a "unified entity." In this case, the 100 block of West Evans, the 100 block of North Dargan, and the 100 block of South Dargan seem to be significant for its association with Florence's commercial development
- A Design Review Board would be created to administer the Design Guidelines and would be inserted into the development plan review and approvals process.
- In addition to the three Zoning Overlay Districts, it is recommended that a Redevelopment Area also be created in downtown Florence, pursuant to Section 6, Chapter 33, of the South Carolina Code. The Section reads in part: "In order to promote and protect the health, safety, morals, and welfare of the public, blighted conditions need to be eradicated and conservation measures instituted, sprawl areas controlled, and redevelopment of such areas undertaken; to remove and alleviate adverse conditions it is necessary to encourage private investment and restore and enhance the tax base of the taxing districts in such areas by the redevelopment of project areas. The eradication of blighted areas and treatment and improvement of sprawl areas and conservation areas by redevelopment projects is declared to be essential to the public interest."
- The Redevelopment Area may provide the City of Florence and Florence County with various management tools, access to incentives, and other benefits pursuant to rights and privileges granted under South Carolina law. Formation of the Redevelopment Area may also serve as the platform for creating a Tax Increment Finance District, also pursuant to Chapter 33 of the South Carolina Code.
- The area referenced as the Redevelopment Area in Florence consists of approximately 500 acres, and is basically bound by Church on the east, Lucas on the north, McQueen, Chase, Kuker, Graham on the west, and Cherokee on the south.
- Formation of the Redevelopment Area will require an amendment to the Consolidated Zoning Ordinance, and its administration and

management structure further defined through an intergovern-
mental agreement. It is anticipated that the Florence Downtown
Development Corporation would be the primary management
entity for administration of the Redevelopment Area. It is further anticipated that the FDDC and its role would be augmented
through the addition of a full-time, professional planner who,
as City staff, would act to implement the Design Guidelines associated with the redevelopment efforts, provide code enforcement
support, and act in various capacities as needed to assist in the
overall redevelopment effort.

- In the future, the City of Florence should pursue the formation
  of a National Register Historic District to afford redevelopment
  projects a combination of federal and state tax incentives,
  and formation of a Municipal Improvement District to focus
  resources on "clean and safe" programs as well as marketing,
  special events, and promotional activity that can benefit merchants and property owners.

Phase I work also led to the following further recommendations:

A. Overlay District Context

The impetus for creating some type of overlay district in downtown
Florence emerged from work done by HDR on the Downtown Master
Plan & City Wide Structure Plan, Community Builders and the Florence
Downtown Development Corporation, the Design Committee, and the
underlying issues and opportunities that these and other entities have
sought to address.

At the outset of the Hunter Interests team work program, there was
a clear expectation that a Zoning Overlay District would be created in
order to implement a set of Design Guidelines that the team would also
prepare. Beyond this, other options were to be explored, and in fact,
during the course of work, the need and/or desire for additional func-
tions were demonstrated.

There is a generally expressed desire for the District to provide
additional "management" control by the City of Florence and/or the
Florence Downtown Development Corporation in order to facilitate
and expedite revitalization efforts. Beyond this, there has also been

discussion of even greater City control being exerted at some point in the future, perhaps under the purview of a newly created City Planning Department. Going even further, some stakeholders have suggested that a City Planning Commission be formed, and that zoning and development regulations would be created and enforced accordingly. These and other layers of planning, governance, and regulation are all theoretically possible, and the team has explored various options at length.

Hunter Interests views the development of the Zoning Overlay District, and other revitalizing bodies, as a phased process that should begin with constructing a strong foundation. The outline of this process is summarized below in District Recommendations.

B. Zoning Overlay District Recommendations

An application for legislative change must be filed by an eligible party (Planning Commission or Council of Jurisdiction) pursuant to Article 9 of the Consolidated Zoning Ordinance. Adopt an amendment to the Consolidated Zoning Ordinance that would create new zoning classifications as follows:

D-1 Downtown Central District: The intent of this district is to promote good urban design, and to establish and maintain a unified, improved identity for downtown Florence, pursuant to the Design Guidelines that would become an additional section, or sub-section, of the Consolidated Zoning Ordinance.

D-2 Downtown Arts and Cultural District: The intent of this district is to promote good urban design, and to build on the attractive and significant architecture that exists through new infill development, and in and through administration of the Design Guidelines that would become an additional section, or sub-section, of the Consolidated Zoning Ordinance.

H-1 Historic District: The intent of this district is to respect and build on the historic character of downtown Florence, and to establish the parameters for pursuit of National Register Historic District designation. This zoning classification would also be subject to the Design Guidelines as adopted into the Consolidated Zoning Ordinance.

The boundaries of these Zoning Overlay Districts are pursuant to the map shown in the Design Guidelines, and are consistent with implementation of the Downtown Master Plan & City-wide structure plan.

The team recommends that once the Zoning Overlay Districts are formed, the City implement a phased program that would be highlighted as follows:

- Design Guidelines are to be mandatory.
- Hire professional planner as staff to oversee implementation and code adherence.
- Create design review board.

Finally, Hunters Interest reviewed financial incentives available for the city and investors.

The Phase II report was also assisted by the architectural firm Allison Platt and Associates of Baltimore, Maryland, and was presented on May 12, 2005.

The Phase II work program and associated results further builds on the public outreach and community involvement process that goes back several years in Florence, and which was accentuated by the consulting team and the FDDC in Phase I. This process has yielded a vibrant vision for the future of Downtown Florence, one that is reflected in the Master Illustrative Site Plan contained in this report and the associated catalyst projects and physical improvements that are recommended. The recommendations contained in this Phase II report are not, however, the product of vision plan or community wish list alone. Rather, they are the result of applying market analysis, financial feasibility analysis, creative yet practical urban design elements, and the consulting team's national experience in downtown revitalization to the issues and opportunities at hand. Phasing, leveraging, land-use and property ownership dynamics, the status of proposed projects, public policy, and the key role of the private sector in the revitalization process have all been carefully taken into consideration.

Thanks to Mayor Frank Willis, the board and staff of the Florence Downtown Development Corporation, the City of Florence staff, the Florence City Council, all stakeholders within the business, civic, and cultural communities and the people of Florence at large, for their help in making Phase II of the Downtown Florence Revitalization Strategy a meaningful step toward a bright future.

The Phase II report then went on to describe, analyze the economics, and position potential downtown projects including offices, mixed-use space, grocery, business incubator, residential space, parking, performing arts center, Little Theatre, Florence Museum, and hotel. The Phase III report was presented in March of 2006.

During 2005, the Hunter Interests team worked with the Florence Downtown Development Commission and the City of Florence to assist in moving forward with Phase III of the Downtown Revitalization Strategy. This phase of the work program involved moving into implementation of various plans and programs recommended in Phases I and II. The FDDC and the City have reason to be proud of their accomplishments in a relatively short period of time. These accomplishments include:

- Completion and approval of the Downtown Revitalization Strategy and Plan—The Phase I report, the initial Downtown Revitalization Strategy, was completed in August 2004. It presented a set of implementation actions, Design Guidelines, and recommendation for the Overlay Zoning Districts in which they would be applied.
- Completion of the redevelopment overlay district—This district defines redevelopment areas for short- and long-term action, and encourages property owners to take such actions.
- Adoption of zoning overlay districts—Three Zoning Overlay Districts were adopted as amendments to the Consolidated Zoning Ordinance. These districts clarify and facilitate specific revitalization activities that otherwise may be precluded by zoning regulations.

After input from FDDC, the City, and citizens/stakeholders, the Design Guidelines were adopted. These guidelines will provide focus and direction for the revitalization of downtown Florence for years to come.

- Preparation and public approval of the streetscape design— Subsequent to approval of the general Design Guidelines, specific designs were prepared and approved for such items as street lighting, trash receptacles, and furniture.

- Preparation and review of streetscape design development drawings—Drawings such as these are an important part of communicating the vision for the appearance of the revitalized downtown area to citizens as well as prospective developers. They include specific proposals for street furniture, roadway improvements, and plantings.

- Preparation of detailed design plan for the breezeway—A detailed plan was developed for the breezeway, a property acquired by the City and planned as a walk-through park connecting parking in the interior of the block with the Evans Street retail area.

- Preparation of a three-dimensional fly-through of designs— The flythrough presentation expands upon the two-dimensional drawings and provides the community with an enhanced vision of the revitalized downtown area. This type of presentation is also useful for encouraging developers and financiers and communicating the desires of the community.

- Updating and completing the historic district survey and data— A survey of the buildings in downtown Florence was completed by the architectural historian on the Hunter Interests team. A minor adjustment in the survey was necessitated by the demolition of a building of potentially historic value. This step was necessary prior to submitting application for National Register Historic District designation.

- Preparation and filing of the initial submission for Historic District designation—The preliminary submission was filed on January 27, 2006. The results of the Preliminary Information Form filing generally take between 30 and 60 days, so the results of the application are expected in April. The entire application process takes between nine and 12 months. See Appendix III for a copy of the submission.

- Initial discussions for an important public finance component— The formation of a Redevelopment District serves as a precursor to a Tax Increment Finance District.

- Technical analysis and projections for the Tax Increment Finance District—The Revitalization Strategy proposed a Tax Increment Finance District to provide a source of public funding for capital improvements for the downtown. Initial projections of potential TIF revenues were completed.

- Finalizing catalyst project land and parking requirements—
The choice of initial projects that create interest and excitement in
a downtown area preparing for revitalization is an important early
step in the process. This was accomplished, and both parking and
land requirements were estimated. These projects will change the
perception of the area to one of a dynamic and desirable place to be.
- Funding commitments for two performing arts facilities—One
of the most important milestones that was accomplished during
Phase III work was the funding commitments. Commitments were
made by the Doctors Bruce and Lee Foundation to fund the Florence Little Theater and the Florence Center for the Arts.
- Preparation of the developer RFP and preliminary mailing list—
Hunter Interests prepared an RFP to solicit parties interested
in developing and/or operating various projects in downtown
Florence, and prepared an initial list of qualified regional and
national developers.
- Interviewing two developer prospects and reviewing their initial
design plans for the first catalyst project—During the course of
this Phase, the Hunter team, the FDDC, and the City all made
overtures to those deemed to have an interest in the various projects in the revitalization plan. Two developers were identified and
interviewed.
- Designation of a development team and prime tenant for the first
and largest catalyst development project—A unique and unprece-
dented mixed use building up to 60,000 square feet is being
aggressively pursued with a designated development team with a
prime tenant who is poised to lease 50% or more of the space.
- Initial negotiations with the catalyst project developer—Another
significant milestone in this work process was the initial negotiations with the designated development team and prime tenant for
the catalyst mixed use development. On a necessarily short time
table, this work is continuing as we move into Phase

- IV.
Agreement on an appropriate transition role for FDDC—As the
downtown Florence revitalization work continues, the Florence
Downtown Development Commission is retaining and expanding

its important role, moving from a strategic planning function into a negotiation and development.

The Hunter Interests group made a follow-up presentation in August 2009 wherein they recorded progress to date and further advice about the designation of the Downtown Historic District which was accomplished with some help by US Senator Lindsey Graham working with Senator Hugh Leatherman. They envisioned the adoption of the City of Florence Master Plan which was accomplished in 2010 (see "Visions 2010" chapter).

The Drs. Bruce and Lee Foundation continued to play an important role in Downtown Florence development. In 2004, they committed $10.6 million to the new Drs. Bruce and Lee Florence County Library; in 2005, they began a four-year commitment to the new Florence Little Theatre of $10.5 million; in 2005, they committed $500,000 to clean up and purchase the future HopeHealth Clinic's site; in 2005, they also spent $300,000 to purchase the old Kress building; also in 2005, they committed to spending $18.2 million toward the FMU Performing Arts Center; in 2011, they committed $2.1 million to the new Barnes Basketball arena; in 2012. they spent $6.5 million to relocate and up-fit city hall; in 2013, they spent $7.3 million toward a new Florence County Museum of the Fine Arts and collections; and in 2014, they committed at least $12.5 million to a new Health Sciences building for FMU in Downtown Florence.

Private investments in Downtown Florence also include about $47 million of investment announced or given as of 2015. The private investors include: about $1.5 million from Coffea Enterprises (Dr. Keith's real estate and restaurants running along the eastern side of Coit Street); about $7 million from Downtown Hospitality Group (headed up by the Holland and Raines families with others); about $4 million from Waters Building; Victors Bistro (the Norwoods); about $2 million from 100 West Evans; about $2.5 million from Med-Enroll (Jimmy Brown, Frank Chisholm, and Tim Norwood); about $11 million from New Florence Development (headed up by Ken Jackson, Ken Ard, and Dale Barth with others); about $4 million from Carolina Bank; about $9 million from Lat Purcer Associates; about $1 million from 155 Dargan; and about $4 million from Stokes Eye

Center. There is about $20 million in further development pending. In addition, various landlords have spent about $2 million on infrastructure improvement.

Other investments from the city and county governments and the State of South Carolina are also important and add about another $70 million to the total, making it about $200 million so far invested in the new Downtown Florence.

Both HDR and Hunter Interests suggested anchor events to stimulate interest in and bring traffic to downtown. Those events have blossomed and proven a great success. On the third Thursday of each month, the Florence Downtown Development Corporation (FDDC), Dolce Vita, The Library, Wholly Smokin BBQ, Thai House II, and the Clay Pot Coffee Shop host a free concert in the William H. Johnson Renaissance Dining Courtyard; the band plays from 6 p.m. to 9 p.m. On the final Friday of each month, the FDDC hosts a free concert in the 100 block of South Dargan; the band plays from 6 p.m. to 8:30 p.m. On the first Friday of each month, the FDDC and Victors Bistro host a free concert in the James Allen Plaza located at 109 South Dargan St.; the band plays from 6 p.m. to 9 p.m. and the restaurant is open before and after the event. Each Wednesday from 3 p.m. to 7 p.m., the FDDC hosts the Downtown Farmers Market in the Cultural Garden at 148 South Dargan Street next to Restaurant Row. The market features local produce, seafood, breads, desserts, and crafts from small local farms and crafters in and around the Pee Dee Region. The market season runs from April 1 to August 26 and new vendors are always welcomed. The market now has a more permanent home several blocks over at 200 Sanborn St. with newly constructed permanent sheds, ramps, and storage.

The SC Pecan Festival, now named the SC Pecan Music and Food Festival, is an annual festival held in Downtown Florence. Its nickname remains "Let's Go Nuts." The Pecan Festival was first suggested to FDDC's chair George Jebaily by Pat Gibson-Hye and Jeanne Dowling in about 2002. At first it had only two stages, about 20 Vendors and about 2,500 visitors. The festival now attracts over fifty-thousand residents and visitors to Downtown Florence each year. The festival typically has eight stages of live entertainment, over 250 food & craft vendors, Pecan Cook-off, Classic Car Show, All

Free Kid's Fun Zone, Downtown Farmers Market, Art Trail on Evans, Run and Bike Like a Nut, Sing Like A Nut Vocal Competition, Pecan Classic Corn Hole Tournament, and tons of amusements. Its growth has been phenomenal—the festival evolved from the Fourth of July "Florence Fling" started by Carolyn and Maurice Dake from GE, moving in 2004 to the first Saturday in November. The tremendous growth has been managed and tirelessly promoted by George Jebaily and his committee.

The FDDC has turned to more than just development and solicitation or management of future development. They now are the promotional and public relations arm of the downtown Historic Area and merchants. And they are working smart and creatively. The FDDC puts out weekly newsletters, a daily email alert about downtown events or restaurant specials, and a Facebook page and other social media. They sponsor and develop an important full-page presentation of the weekend's upcoming events in each Thursday issue of the *Morning News*. And finally, they are the problem-solvers and hand-holders for all the downtown interests and participants.

All of Mayor Frank's work on Downtown Florence redevelopment and infrastructure paid off handsomely. Downtown flourished and continues to grow years after Mayor Frank. The water and sewer infrastructure allowed important expansions. The efforts lead to multiple Municipal Achievement Awards for Economic Development from the Municipal Association of South Carolina, including sequential awards from 2013 to 2018.

Historical and editorial assistance came from David Williams, Drew Griffin, George Jebaily, Tom Marschel, and Ray Reich.

Darlington Raceway in action

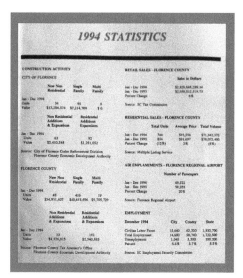

End 1994 Florence economic data

Willis Construction Company office

Honda South Carolina site

The Conway Bypass

Roche Carolina site

The Campaigns

Willis campaign mailer

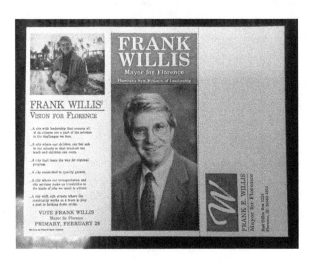

Willis campaign brochure

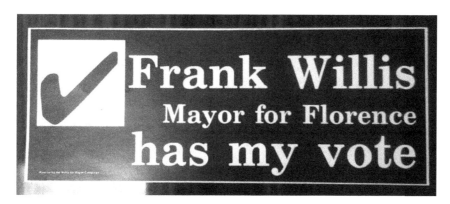

Willis campaign bumper sticker

Mayor Willis takes the oath of office with Brittany and James Schofield

First lot clearing, Church Street

All-American City & Community Award Campaign

Application for All-American City

All-American City campaign logo-sticker

Tom Kinard and Jane Pigg on the radio in Kansas City

Tom Kinard show spoof

Preventing Juvenile Crime

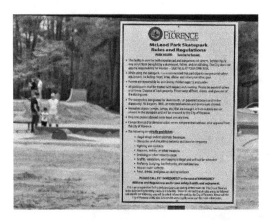 

McLeod Park skate park

The Veterans Park

Florence Veterans Park entrance

Veterans Park opening ceremonies

Colonel Wingard speaks at opening ceremonies

Veterans Park monuments

Veterans Park monuments

Veterans Park Wall of Honor

Circle of Flags, entrance to Florence

Hotel Florence

FDTC downtown Florence campus

Dr. John Keith's Restaurant Row

Columbia Museum of Art

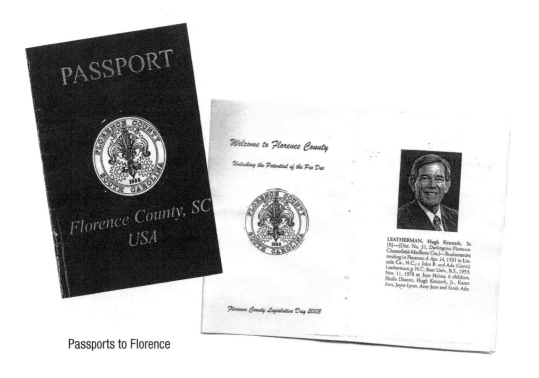

Passports to Florence

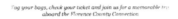

Tag your bags, check your ticket and join us for a memorable trip
aboard the Florence County Connection

We'll be making a stop at the Columbia Museum of Art.
Wednesday, March 31

Come sample our famous Florentine hospitality
and discover how the Florence County Connection is
transporting eastern South Carolina to the future

It will be an evening of entertainment and information
and a journey you'll be glad you experienced!

Florence Legislative Day gifts

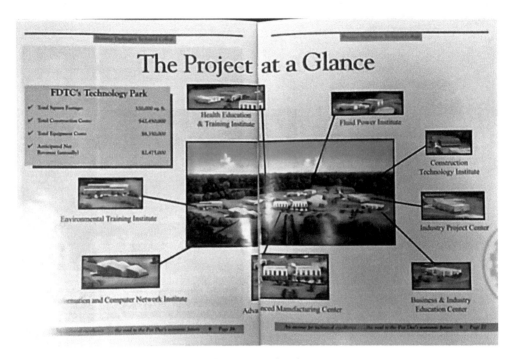

SiMT marketing brochure

SiMT fountain

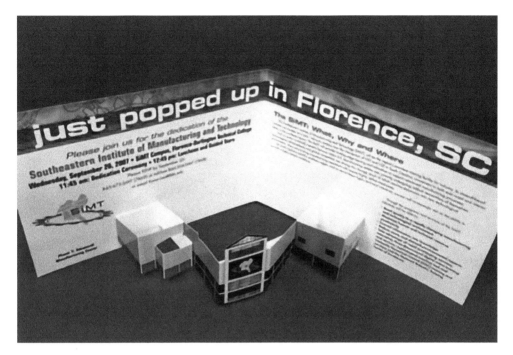

Pop-up marketing piece

SiMT Extension

NESA, then and now

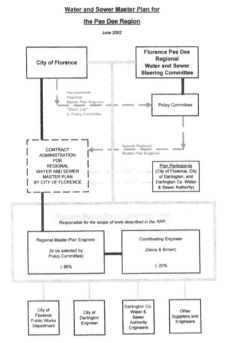

Water planning and organization

Wastewater management facility

Water treatment plant

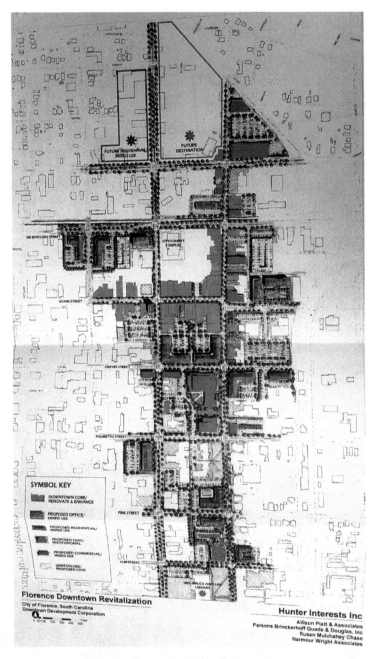

Scope of the downtown development project

An Exceptional Historic Downtown Development Opportunity

Florence, South Carolina

Florence County Library

Florence City/County Civic Center

The photo at left shows the existing view looking east on Evans Street toward the intersection with Dargan. The sketch above illustrates renovation of buildings, signage and streetscapes, and a concept for a new building at the end of the street on Dargan.

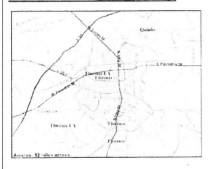

Downtown Florence

Florence Darlington College Allied Health Building

Francis Marion University

HUNTER INTERESTS
I N C O R P O R A T E D

Florence Downtown
Development Corporation

Drs. Bruce and Lee Library

Florence County Museum

Rebuilt Downtown Florence

Florence City Hall

Performing Arts Center

Florence Little Theatre

James Allen Plaza

Drs. Bruce and Lee Foundation original board

Posters used in Performing Arts Center early days

Performing Arts Center

PAC opening week brochure

PAC leadership plaque

The School Foundation logo

The Dr. Eddie Floyd Florence Tennis Complex

Entrance to Dr. Eddie Floyd Tennis Center

Jennie O'Bryan Avenue sign

Tennis courts

Administration and civic building

The Basel Group

The Basel Group wives

Basel map

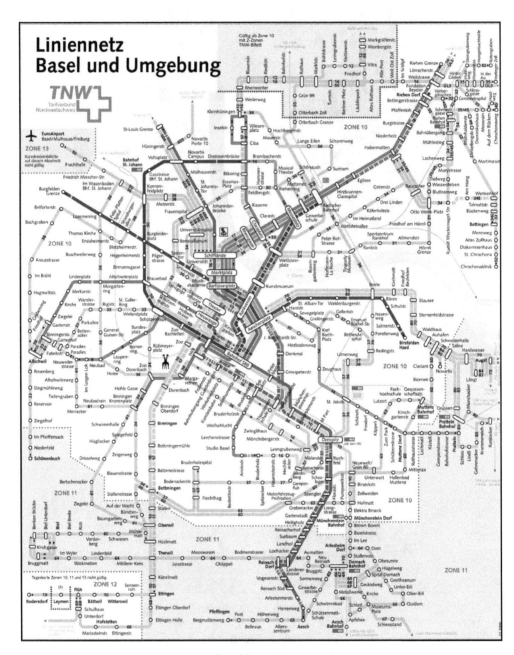

Basel tram system

Restaurant Stucki

Tinguely Fountain

Willi's Cafe

On location

Basel City Hall

Novartis

Roche

Dr. Gould's Basel students

Nufer Clinic

Mayor Nufer

The two mayors

SiMT

Darlington Economic Development office

Fiber Industries site

Florence Center

Pee Dee Pride jersey

Pride marketing sign

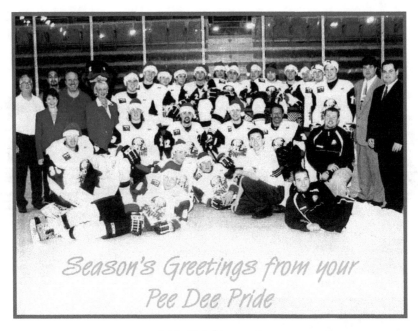

Pride Christmas card

Senator Hugh Leatherman

The Performing Arts Center

THE FRANCIS Marion University Performing Arts Center (PAC) has added depth and sophistication to Florence's downtown development. We once gave a few New Yorkers a mini-tour of Downtown Florence and they were excited by the PAC, saying "We must be in Europe." The architecture is stunning, and the acoustics are ranked in the top three venues across the world. The Mainstage auditorium can seat 849 with a stage that stands 58 feet wide and 38 feet high. It is equipped with an orchestra pit, an automatic orchestra shell, and a fly tower. The Holzman Moss Bottino architects earned well-deserved kudos.

Florence dreamt of an arts center for a long time, even back to the 1960–70s. Vision 2000 asked for a center, saying the time is now. In the 1990s, several groups organized to push a project forward. Key folks at that time were Julia Buyck, Starr Ward, Beverly Hazelwood, Rebecca Greenberg, Shirley Imbeau, Mary Alice Ingram, and Evans Holland. Hurtles remained, including location, how to pay for the construction, and most importantly how to manage it and afford operating costs.

The Florence folks visited several South Carolina arts centers in 2001, including Koger Center (Columbia), Peace Center (Greenville), Patriots Hall (Sumter), Coker Center (Hartsville), and Newberry

Opera House (Newberry). An important town meeting was held in Florence on June 4, 2002, with Judith Allen, president of the Blumenthal Center in Charlotte, North Carolina, who offered encouragement. Some seed money from fundraising events and the Drs. Bruce and Lee Foundation afforded a feasibility study that showed Florence could support a center with up to 1,200 seats and a 300-seat auxiliary theater.

The timing was right to move the project ahead. Senator Hugh Leatherman was now the chair of the South Carolina Senate Finance Committee; the Drs. Bruce and Lee Foundation was in a position to spend significant money in Florence; the mayor and the Foundation had moved Florence Downtown development forward enough for another project; and the new FMU president, Dr. Fred Carter, was ready to move some of campus into the city limits of Florence. Importantly, Dr. Carter was politically connected to all three key funding sources and he, unlike previous FMU presidents, favored coming into Florence. But even so, nothing moved forward overnight.

The community groups and Mayor Frank approached Dr. Carter in 2004 about getting involved. The key piece was that it would be a Francis Marion University building to be managed and operated by the university. During a Carolina Hospital System board retreat, Dr. Carter was able to convince the Drs. Bruce and Lee Foundation leadership to look at funding a portion of the PAC as long as FMU built it and ran it. By 2006, the pieces were falling into place after Dr. Carter's successful lobbying of Mayor Willis, Senator Leatherman, and Dr. Eddie Floyd of the Drs. Bruce and Lee Foundation. The project cost would be spread out among the principals: $18 million from the Drs. Bruce and Lee Foundation, $12 million from the state and $4 million from the city; other contributors included McLeod Hospital, Diamond Plywood, BB&T Bank, and Charles Ingram Lumber. The FMU Board gave final approval to the project on February 4, 2006.

The university organized a Performing Arts Center Governing Board in June 2005: Larry Anderson, Michael Blakeley, Fred Carter, Shirley Imbeau, Marva Smalls, Billy Williams, and Ben Zeigler. Groundbreaking was on January 30, 2009. The grand opening was on September 9, 2011. Nearly a spectacular week of outstanding performances headlined by Roberta Flack and Judy Collins marked the occasion. The architects were Holzman Moss Bottino Architecture (New York) and FW Architects (Florence), and the contractor was MB Kahn Construction (Columbia). The facility was outstanding with astonishing acoustics, one of the three best in the world, according to the architects.

The board began a search for a director in 2007, selecting Laura Sims—of 60 applicants, five were interviewed, and two finalists were called in for second interviews. Laura Sims was educated at Auburn University, the University of Missouri, and the National Endowment for the Arts. She moved from stage manager to production manager from 1993 to 1999 at several facilities, including Hilton Head in South Carolina, and then was manager of a $3 million per year operation at Clarence Brown Theatre in Knoxville, Tennessee. Her first task in Florence was to promote the project around the community and then to work with the architects and consultants on developing the building and classrooms. Laura successfully developed membership growth with great shows and outstanding performers appealing to the key age groups of the Florence community. The current director is A.T. "Bud" Simmons.

Notable performers at the PAC have included Richard Cross, Art Garfunkel, Sally Struthers, and several famous groups; Roberta Flack and Judy Collins were the opening acts on back-to-back nights in 2011. The Florence Symphony Orchestra now calls the PAC home, along with the Masterworks Choir and the South Carolina Dance Theatre. The university also has classrooms, acoustic practice rooms, and halls in the facility.

The board appointed a Performing Arts Center Foundation in 2008: George Beshere, Julia Buyck, Mark Vinson, Beverly Hazelwood, Starr Ward, Paula Lawson, Andrew Kampiziones, and Betty Ann Darby.

Historical assistance came from Beverly Hazelwood and Shirley Imbeau; editorial and historical assistance came from Dr. Fred Carter.

The School Foundation

GRADY GREER was key to the formation of the School Foundation. Grady had worked as assistant district administrator for the public school system of Darlington County for 11 years, from 1960 to 1972. Despite taking over the Florence Toledo Scale franchise in 1972, he maintained a keen interest in public education. In the mid-1980s he worked with the South Carolina State Chamber of Commerce to assist local school districts to raise funds through public or private sources, with the Coalition for Educational Excellence.

Grady worked with business leaders and the members of the Florence Forum, a small group of Florence civic and thought leaders spearheaded by Don Herriott of Roche Carolina and local attorney Steve Wukela. Together, they worked to put on a Special Election in 1999 with a referendum issue of Limited Fiscal Autonomy for the Florence 1 Schools. The measure narrowly lost because of a printing error in the keypunch ballot whereby the usual order of "Yes" and "No" was reversed; legal challenge to repeal the election was not successful.

So, after the referendum defeat, Grady, Don Herriott, Steve Imbeau, and others began to discuss the following idea: we don't want to go through another referendum right now, but given the significant support for the referendum measure by the business community, why not raise the money privately from the businesses that were willing to pay more taxes to support the schools and put that money into a foundation that could hopefully end up doing basically the same thing? The idea gained traction through the Florence Forum and in the business community with the help of Don Herriott from Roche Carolina and Ian Shaw from Wellman, Darlington Plant. Grady got to work with their key assistance to organize the new foundation.

The new organization was called the School Foundation and officially registered with the South Carolina Secretary of State on February 7, 2000, by Don Herriott, Grady Greer, and Steve Wukela. Don Herriott was the first president, Grady the vice president and treasurer, and Steve Wukela the secretary. The early board of trustee meetings were so important that we will cover them in some detail.

The first meeting was on held Tuesday, May 9, 2000, at DuBard Inc. offices; this was a critical and highly accomplished meeting. The new board included Grady Greer, Fred DuBard, Frank Willis, Stephen Imbeau, Don Herriott, Steve Wukela, Trip DuBard, Reamer King, Robert Williams, Tom Ewart, Charlene Lowery, Libby Godbold, Jean Leatherman, Carroll Player, Emerson Gower, Ashby Lowrimore, Frank Avent, Joe Nelson (ex officio), Clotilda Diggs, Tom Levine, and the school board chair (ex officio). Evelyn Heyward was added later. The officers were approved. The mission was outlined by Grady: fund a foundation to support Florence 1 Schools with projects outside the normal budget; make one large grant per year; no grants until $1 million raised; pay expenses from earnings, not principal; and aim for a $10 million corpus in ten years. The proposed bylaws were approved with certain amendments. Committees were organized: finance (Robert Williams, chair); grants (Frank Willis, chair); audit (Tom Levine, chair). Burch Oxer Seale was selected as accountants and a press conference was set for August. Finally, guiding principles were adopted: action and decisions should be clearly linked to student academic achievement and good citizenship, teacher quality, safe/efficient operations, and district leadership; funding should be to enhance costs beyond normal operating expenses; major grants only; foundation operating and overhead expenses were to be kept at absolute minimum level; a diverse foundation board membership should be developed; the foundation exists to benefit all children of

Florence 1 Schools; the foundation should prepare our children for success; and remember, it's about the children, not the foundation.

The follow-up meeting was on September 13, 2000. Already, outside clerical work was needed. Trip DuBard and Emerson Gower had developed an aggressive fundraising plan: contact the Drs. Bruce and Lee Foundation, contact potential large donors, and develop a solicitation packet. In addition to an initial $100,000 investment, Roche Carolina committed to matching grants of up to $100,000 for three years.

A kickoff breakfast was scheduled for November 15, 2000, at the Roche Carolina entrance hall for the School Foundation board, the School Board, and the community—speakers included Stephen Imbeau (master of ceremonies), Don Herriott, Representative Jim Clyburn, Trip DuBard, Grady Greer, and Fred DuBard. The trustees agreed to organize a contest for the foundation logo, and Rick Reames would coordinate with the district art coordinator and the district art teachers. Grady personally offered a $400 prize for a logo design contest.

By the February 27, 2001, board meeting, the foundation had some money in the bank, as reported by Grady: $317, 776.20. Most of the meeting was taken up with fundraising planning as reported by Trip DuBard: corporate donations solicited by board members, commercials to be run in March and April as supplied by Hartnett and Foster, a website in production by Hill South (*theschoolfoundation .org*), advertising billboards donated by DuBard Inc. and Adams Outdoor Advertising, and several other fundraising ideas. It was decided the foundation would host the first fundraising gala in 2002. By August 27, the fund was beyond $458,000. Once again, the bulk of the August meeting was for discussion of fundraising and marketing. The goal of $1 million was set for the end of the year and the gala event was set for May.

The gala was the main topic of the January 16, 2002, board meeting. David Wach, IT manager at Roche Carolina, volunteered to chair the event, now changed to September 19; David continued as gala manager until about 2008. After discussion, the board decided to allow for a pass-through grant so the foundation could make an award at the Gala of up to $50,000. By the May 2, 2002, meeting, the fund was up to $576,000 and ready for a marketing campaign. Mark Wilson was coming out with a new slogan ("For our Children, for our Future") for billboards and other media. The web page was updated to reflect the changes. Working with David Wach, Trip DuBard began taking an active role in the first gala. Student talent would be highlighted, chosen from across the district; tables would be sold, and sponsors solicited; Darla Moore (a businesswoman, financier, and philanthropist born in Lake City) would be the first featured speaker and Marva Smalls (the executive vice president at Nickelodeon and human resources for MTV) would be the distinguished graduate. Marva has continued to rise at Viacom and is now involved in its global management. The meeting ended with discussion of grant procedures and how to select the grant recipients across Florence 1 Schools. Gala meetings were held on June 13 and June 27; a silent auction was added to the gala's program of events. Pass-through grants were approved of $15,000 (the money donated by Roche Carolina and Carolina Power & Light) to the Montessori Program and North Vista Elementary School, and a $10,000 grant was suggested for Royall Elementary School.

By the meeting on December 18, 2002, the foundation was very close to its $1 million goal with almost $800,000. The first gala was a great success and already tables had been reserved for the next year's event, on September 9, 2003. The 2002 event netted about $160,000 for the foundation. By the April 23, 2003, meeting, the program was already set for the September 9, 2003, gala with featured speaker Marion Wright Edelman and distinguished graduate Judge David Harwell. Ian Shaw and Frank Bullard were added to the board. Discussions were begun to bring on part-time or contract staff. The board realized that the grant process needed a more formal structure. The retiring board members in 2003—Carroll Player, Robert Williams, and Tom Levine—were replaced by Tom Stanton, James Byrd, and Kanti Patel.

The 2003 gala netted nearly $150,000 for the foundation and the September 23, 2004, gala would feature speaker Jerry Richardson and distinguished graduate Harry Carson. Discussion of a contact fundraiser was initiated. Rick Reames at the district worked out a grant process acceptable to most: 1) formal grant requests from across the district would go to the district office; 2) applications would be ranked by district with a grants committee of six people, two not employed by the district; 3) all ranked applications would then be sent to the school board who would then send on to the School Foundation grants committee their selection for award; 4) and the foundation will make the final determination based on merit and available funds. Jean Leatherman was asked to continue to fine-tune the grants process and procedures. The investment committee was also reformulated with Fred DuBard as chair and members Reamer King, Ian Shaw, and adviser Bradley Callicott (from the Drs. Bruce and Lee Foundation).

Big changes were coming to the foundation by the December 8, 2004, board meeting. The Foundation had gone well over the $1 million amount with about $1.3 million. Don Herriott resigned as he was soon to become one of the international -production managers for Roche Carolina. Trip DuBard was elected president to take Don Herriott's prestigious place—big shoes to replace, for sure. Trip immediately added two new committees—PR/marketing and operations—and realigned the board to only members who would take active roles in the foundation's operations. Over the next six months, several members rotated off the School Foundation board.

Trip aggressively grew the foundation. In fact, it almost became Trip DuBard's life, as he was both chair and executive director, all without pay. He stayed on until 2008. Trip particularly has fond memories of three of the galas: 2004 with Harry Carson and a football theme, 2005 with Allie Brooks and a school campus and gymnasium theme, and 2006 with Ann "Tunky" Riley and a political theme including an election decided by hanging chads. Trip and his board began to realize that the Foundation needed professional management.

Trip DuBard hired Debbie Hyler in 2006 as executive director. Debbie had managed several businesses: her husband's medical practice; a small real estate company (owned by her family, Mark Steadman, and Steve Imbeau); and business and operations manager of the Pee Dee Pride hockey team (owned by Fred DuBard, the Hylers, and Steve Imbeau—previous local owners of the hockey team included Jean Leatherman, Frank Avent, and Marguerite Willis). Debbie was also active in political fundraising. She was an excellent pick: dynamic, thorough, detail-oriented, personable, an excellent public speaker, and good on her feet. She immediately established rigorous accounting procedures, more frequent board meetings, professional public relations, yearly planning retreats, and changed the grant amounts to 4 percent of the Foundation Corpus plus half of the net funds raised in the target year. She continues as the director.

Debbie added another event in 2006 with the help of Harry Carson and his football and golfing friends; the Harry Carson Celebrity Golf Classic held at the Country Club of South Carolina. The event was a lot of fun, bringing a lot of celebrities into Florence, but it was also a lot of work and was discontinued after the second year. The net proceeds did not justify the work. Many of us worked the tournament as volunteers out on the course or off the tee.

Under Debbie, the board meetings followed a routine agenda with the finance/fundraising, investment management, grants, PR and marketing, director's report, and chair's report. By 2008, Jeff Helton (Honda) was the chair, and in 2011 Ian Shaw assumed the role, but as Wellman was shut down shortly after, he resigned with brief service, returning Jeff Helton to office. The biggest development in 2011 was the development of a new spring event beginning in 2012, the "Dancing with the Stars" fundraiser promoted by Debbie Hyler, Jean Leatherman, and Mindy Taylor. The event was modeled after the popular TV show and was immediately a big hit in Florence with fierce competition, all good for the cause of the foundation.

The School Foundation continues to grow and prosper. The Dancing with the Stars gala has outshone the fall gala, but the fall event is necessary to highlight the work of the school and the foundation. The corpus is now over $2 million, and the grant totals now are at $1.2 million—a very good ratio given the restraints on the fund balance and use of funds; small grants are not included in this global number.

Current leaders of the foundation (as of 2021) include Jeff Helton as chair and Courtney Cribb as treasurer. Debbie Hyler remains director has an assistant, Beverly McKee. Board members include Annie Brown, Trisha Caulder, Bobbie Chowdhary, Brooke Evans, Marion Ford, Keisha Johnson, Dr. Charlie Jordan, Ed Love, Beverly McGee, Tammy Pawloski, James Sheehy, Lissa Raison, Jeff Stevens, Porter Stewart, Mindy Taylor, Brent Tiller, and Carlos Washington.

Historical and editorial assistance came from Don Herriott, Trip DuBard, Debbie Hyler, and foundation staff.

SCHOOL FOUNDATION GALA EVENTS

YEAR	AMOUNT RAISED	FEATURED SPEAKER	DISTINGUISHED GRADUATE
2002	$160,000	Darla Moore	Marva Smalls
2003	$150,000	Marion Wright Edelman	Judge David Harwell
2004	$100,000	Jerry Richardson	Harry Carson
2005	$86,000		Dr. Allie Brooks
2006	$75,000	Senator Lindsey Graham	Ann "Tunky" Riley
2007	$103,000	Dr. Benjamin Dunlap	Representative Ed Young
2008	$95,000	William Milliken	Jolette Law
2009	$56,000	General Richard Myers	Lieutenant General Charles Bagnal
2010	$96,000	Donald Fehr	Reggie Sanders
2011	$63,000		Mark Walberg
2012	$66,000	Dr. Gerrita Postlewait	Nick Zeigler
2013	$66,000		Hunter Lingle Bell
2014	$69,000		William Hubbard
2015	$68,000		Ben Ingram
2016	$76,000		Stephen Wukela
2017	$40,000		Gerald Evans
2018	$50,000		Waymond Mumford
2019	$57,000		Nancy Snowden
2020	No event (COVID-19)		

DANCING WITH THE STARS EVENTS

YEAR	NET RAISED
2011	$40,000
2012	$110,000
2013	$141,000
2014	$157,000
2015	$149,000
2016	$135,000
2017	$123,000
2018	$123,000
2019	$97,000

MAJOR GRANTS

YEAR	AMOUNT	PROJECT NAME	SCHOOL(S) INVOLVED	GRANT WRITER
2002	$25,000	Elementary Instruction	Royall, North Vista	FSD1 Administration
2005–06	$37,000	LEAP Labs	Timrod, Briggs, Wallace Gregg	Edwina Faulkenberry
2006–07	$71,500	Creative Economy	All middle and high schools	Laura Greenway
2007–08	$109,000	Mechatronics and Health Science	Florence Career Center	Jim Shaw
2008–09	$90,000	Bridging the Divide	DL Carter, Southside, South Florence	Liz Collins
2008–09	$5,000	Mini Grants	Various schools	
2008–09	$25,000	FSD1 Needs Assessment	All schools in FSD1	
2009–10	$50,000	Math Masters of the Pee Dee	All elementary schools	Ginger Baggette
2009–10	$4,198.20	Mini Grants	Various schools	
2010–11	$4,962.54	Mini Grants	Various schools	
2010–11	$96,740.38	Major Grants (4)		
2011–12	$95,332.42	Major Grants (4) 11 Mini Grants	Various schools	
2012–13	$97,405.89	Major Grants (3) 8 Mini Grants	Various Schools	
2013–14	$99,440.79	Major Grants (4) 2 Mini Grants	Various schools	
2014–15	$151,771.93	Major Grants (2) 5 Mini Major Grants	Various Schools	
2015–16	$129,003.61	Major Grants (2) 5 Mini		
2016–17	$114,000	Major Grants (4) 5 Mini Grants		
2017–18	$150,000	Major Grants (4) 5 Mini Grants		
2018–19	$170,000	Major Grants (5)		
2019–20	$145,000	Major Grants (6)		
End of 2020	$1,714,444	TOTAL IN GRANTS		
End of 2020	$2,475,950	FUND BALANCE		

The Dr. Eddie Floyd
Florence Tennis Complex

THE STORY of the major tennis court project on the west side of Florence is really the story of Jennie O'Bryan and the Florence Tennis Association (FTA), the spark plugs behind this successful project started during Mayor Frank's term, with his full support, and finished under Mayor Stephen Wukela. The 2021 leadership of the FTA (*thefta.com*) includes Kevin Light, Ernie James, Ronelle Vanheerden, and Brian Huggins. Jennie served on Florence County Council from 2003 to 2006. Over the years, Jennie and her husband, prominent internist Conyers O'Bryan (co-founder of Pee Dee Internal Medicine Associates) were close to Dr. Eddie Floyd and his wife Kay; Dr. Floyd was a local surgeon, businessman, entrepreneur, philanthropist, and large landowner. The two men were both distant relatives and school roommates, forming a lifelong bond, particularly since they practiced medicine in the same small town within 30 miles of their birthplaces. Jennie was thus able to talk with Dr. Floyd more easily than most, since obviously moving in the same social circles, including being members of the same supper club, the Wine Club. The Wine Club was made famous and feasible through the expertise and extensive wine collections of both Drs. Roy Skinner and Conyers O'Bryan and the excellent chiefs of the Florence Country Club.

DR. EDDIE FLOYD FLORENCE TENNIS CENTER
Report by the City of Florence to the Drs. Bruce and Lee Foundation
January 18, 2012

The City of Florence held the ribbon cutting and grand opening of the newly constructed Dr. Eddie Floyd Florence Tennis Center on Wednesday, July 20, 2011. After the opening ceremonies, a variety of tennis activities and events were scheduled at the Florence Tennis Center throughout the afternoon and evening.

The Florence Tennis Center features 24 asphalt courts, 6 Har-Tru clay courts and a tennis activity center with outdoor decking for a total of 30 courts. The activity center also includes a lounge area, student study area, restrooms, locker rooms, meeting and office space and a pro shop. The Tennis Center is located at 1060 North Cashua Drive. The location of the facility is ideally situated for easy access and participation by all members of the Florence community. This complex will host league play, open/free play, special instruction, and developmental tennis clinics. In partnership with the Florence Tennis Association, the City also plans to develop an after-school educational/tennis outreach program for city youth.

Initial site design and engineering for the tennis complex was performed by URS-B.P. Barber Engineering. Construction on the tennis complex site was done by Kirven Construction with asphalt court construction by Talbot Tennis. Construction on the clay courts was done by Welch Tennis Courts, Inc. The City selected Collins/Almers Architecture to provide architectural design for the Tennis Activity Center and construction of the Tennis Activity Center was performed by Loveless Commercial Contracting, Inc.

Funding sources for the Florence Tennis Center include:

City of Florence	$3,074,000	Construction
County of Florence	$522,000	Access Road
Drs. Bruce and Lee Foundation	$1,500,000	Tennis Activity Center
	$500,000	Clay Courts
Dr. C. Edward Floyd	$535,000	Land Donation (25 acres)
Nucor	$69,800	Land Donation (3 acres)

Since the opening of the Tennis Center in July, the City of Florence Parks and Beautification Department has been productive in promoting and marketing the new center through several programs and events. Weekly scheduled programs include various adult and youth related clinics and lessons such as Cardio Tennis, Adult Academy, Fahrenheit High Performance Academy (youth), and Junior Team Tennis. Individual and Group Lessons are able to be purchased through the Tennis Director.

We look forward to expanding tennis in the Florence Community and surrounding areas through the Dr. Eddie Floyd Florence Tennis Center! It is essential that we strive to develop diverse programs and recruit quality tournaments.

The timeline of the entire project from the City of Florence files is provided by Amanda Pope.

June 2006–Florence Tennis Association (FTA) begins discussions with the City of Florence and Florence County regarding the possibility of constructing a 30 court tennis complex. Members of the FTA approach Dr. C. Edward Floyd about the possibility of a land donation for the tennis center on the old Clemson property located between Hwy. 52 (Lucas Street) and North Cashua Drive and NUCOR about the possibility of a land donation adjacent to the Nucor Credit Union for a public access road to the tennis complex site.

August 21, 2006–Florence Tennis Association makes a presentation and request for consideration to City Council for the construction and operation of a 30 court tennis complex. Florence County Councilmember Jennie O'Bryan, attending the meeting on behalf of the FTA, stated that she had contacted Dr. Floyd about the project and the possible donation of land. She also stated that the County has agreed to assist with the access road and infrastructure on the project. Councilmember O'Bryan also stated that the County had applied for a Drs. Bruce & Lee Foundation grant to assist in moving this project forward. City Council approved a motion for City staff to move forward with a feasibility study for the construction and operation of a tennis complex.

September 28, 2006–Request for Proposals due from qualified consulting firms to the City for master plan and design services of a 30 court tennis complex.

October 19, 2006–Florence County assigns to the City of Florence rights to accept Deed of Gift for 15 acres of property donated by Dr. C. Edward Floyd and 3 acres of property donated by Nucor/Vulcraft Group.

December 7, 2006–Florence County, at the request of Councilmember Jennie O'Bryan, approves to commit funds in the amount of $522,000 to the City of Florence for the construction of a public access road and water/sewer extension along this road for the tennis complex.

December 4, 2006–City of Florence submits grant application to the Drs. Bruce & Lee Foundation in the amount of $44,000 to be used to contract with a consulting firm for master plan and design services including cost estimates for a 30 court tennis complex.

December 18, 2006–City of Florence contracts with Wood+Partners, Inc. for consulting services relating to the master plan and design services of a 30 court tennis complex.

May 14, 2007–WPi, Inc. present preliminary report to City staff and FTA representations for master plan layout and cost estimates. The cost estimate for the 30 tennis court layout including activity center and access road to the tennis center site was $6.8M

October 2007–WPi, Inc. final report completed.

October 2007–City staff, along with representatives from the FTA, review, reduce and revise project construction cost to more accurately reflect an amount for possible funding sources. With reductions in some areas of original cost estimate the projected construction cost for a 24 court complex including a tennis activity center and access road is $5M

January 2008–City and FTA meet with Dr. Floyd and NUCOR to discuss donations of land for tennis complex and access road to tennis complex site.

Spring 2008–City staff puts together a budget for the tennis complex project and possible funding sources for presentation to City Council for consideration.

Summer 2008–City Council approves funding mechanism for tennis complex.

Summer 2008–City staff negotiates professional services agreement with BP Barber to provide engineering services related to the planning, design, preparation of contract documents, permitting and construction administration for the proposed access road and tennis complex.

September 12, 2008–City staff and FTA make presentation to Drs. Bruce & Lee Foundation committee regarding the proposed tennis complex and request grant in the amount of $1.5M for the construction of a tennis activity center.

Fall 2008–BP Barber prepares specifications for access road and tennis complex. Access road to be publicly bid for construction and bids are due back to the City on December 16, 2008. Specifications for the construction of the tennis complex are close to completion and are scheduled to be publicly bid in late January 2009.

November 2008–The City of Florence prepares formal grant request to the Drs. Bruce & Lee Foundation in the amount of $1.5M for the construction of a tennis activity center along with the 24 court tennis complex.

February 2009–Architectural design of the Tennis Activity Center publicly advertised for bid.

March 18, 2009–The City of Florence has selected Collins & Associates of Florence as the design architect for the tennis activity center which will be a part of the new Tennis Complex. The City received over twenty submittals for architectural design services of this facility and through a selection process the project design was awarded to Collins & Associates. The tennis activity center will be designed for approximately ± 7000 SF with outdoor decking and patio areas. The center will also include a lounge area, student study area, locker rooms, restrooms, meeting and office space and a pro shop.

Construction on the access road for the tennis center site is scheduled to begin at the end of March. Final design and specifications for the tennis complex are being completed at this time and should be publicly bid in April 2009. In the next couple of months, the City will also be working with Collins & Associates for the design and building specifications of the activity center in order that they may be publicly bid in August 2009. The anticipated project completion date will be March 2010.

April 2009–Final design specifications and bid documents advertised for construction—contract for construction awarded to Kirven Construction.

May 2009–Goodson Construction awarded contract for the construction of an access road to the Florence Tennis Complex site.

November 2009–Kirven Construction begins construction on the Florence Tennis Complex site.

February 2010–The unusual amount and frequency of rainfall over the last several months has created significant issues and slowed construction efforts for both Goodson Construction on the access road and Kirven Construction on the tennis complex site. Drainage outfalls from both the access road and tennis complex have been unable to handle the amounts of water on the site causing even wetter conditions and limiting the amount of construction that has been able to be completed to date. City staff and B.P. Barber Engineers have gained permission from adjacent landowners to allow Goodson Construction to clear and re-grade several outfall ditches around the complex area. This re-grading should allow ponding water on both the access road and the complex site to drain and both sites to begin to dry out in order that construction may resume. At the same time, Kirven Construction will create an additional service entrance on the east side of the complex site so that as soon as the site is dry enough they can begin to get supplies and equipment back to work on the tennis site while Goodson Construction continues to stabilize the access road.

February 2010–Construction progress by Goodson Construction and Kirven Construction on both the Florence Tennis Center access road and court site continues to be hampered by the frequency of rainfall. In the last two weeks, Florence received two days of rain as well as 3.5 inches of snow. Drainage outfall ditches for the access road and tennis complex are continuing to be cleared and re-graded to allow ponding water on both the access road and the complex site to drain off of the construction sites. Kirven Construction plans to create an additional service entrance on the east side of the tennis complex property as soon as possible in order to get supplies and equipment back to the complex site and resume work.

April 8, 2010–Site work and construction is again underway on the Florence Tennis Complex. The weather has been great the past ten days and the lack of rain coupled with the sunshine and warmer temperatures has allowed a considerable amount of ponding water on site to evaporate. Kirven Construction has completed construction on the temporary access road on the eastern side of the property and is now on site working on the construction of the stormwater retention pond. The site contractor is also removing or "mucking out" poor soil in several areas on site and replacing this soil with better sand clay in preparation of the pads for the tennis courts. It is anticipated that Goodson Construction will be able to complete the improvements for the drainage ditches on adjacent properties next week so they can get back to work on the access road. The Tennis Activity Building has also been publicly advertised and bids for the construction of this facility are scheduled to be opened on April 21, 2010.

April 2010–Tennis Activity Center—Proposed Building Specifications
Construction Budget = $1,500,000 to include architectural design fee
Building Size = ± 5000 SF
Generalities = Two story building with second floor outdoor patio and decking around sides and back of building
First Floor = Entrance with large open area to include lounge area, student study area with computers, tennis pro office and pro shop area, staff office space, elevator, storage area(s), men's and women's locker room facility with access from inside or outside, janitorial closet(s) with storage space and storage area with access from outside for blowers, brooms, etc.
Second Floor = Large open meeting space, office and storage space, concessions area for serving during tournaments, etc. (hospitality area), smaller meeting space, restrooms and access to outdoor patio and decking areas.

This tennis complex will serve as the home facility for the Florence Tennis Association, hosting league play, open/free play, special instruction and developmental tennis camps and clinics. The Association would also like to develop an after-school educational/tennis outreach program for city youth. The Florence Tennis Association is an all volunteer non-profit organization with over 300 members that is committed to promoting recreational tennis as a healthful, family-oriented sport. They conduct and sponsor a variety of adult and junior tournaments, leagues, and youth activities and work closely with the local governments to keep the public courts in good shape.

June 2010–Loveless Commercial Contracting, Inc. hired as the contractor for the construction of the Tennis Activity Center.

July 22, 2010–Site work and construction is moving forward on the Florence Tennis Complex. Kirven Construction has substantially completed construction on the stormwater retention pond and has six of the twenty-four courts graded and covered with a stone base. The electrical contractor is also in the process of installing lights on several of the courts as the site contractor preps these areas for paving. Goodson Construction has completed improvements for the drainage ditches on adjacent properties and has also added crushed stone to the access road. RWF Construction, LLC is now working on the sewer lift station that will be constructed on the northeast corner of the tennis property. Progress Energy is in the process of running power along the access road from Cashua Drive to the Tennis Complex. The contracts for construction of the Tennis Activity Building have been signed with Loveless Commercial Contracting, Inc. of Cayce, SC and they have submitted information to Florence County for the building permits which Loveless hopes to have in about a week at which time they would begin mobilizing equipment and supplies to the site for construction.

August 2010–Tennis Activity Center construction began.

February 2011–The City of Florence begins interview process for tennis coordinator position for the new Florence Tennis Complex. Candidates will be interviewed by City staff as well as three representatives from the Florence Tennis Association.

June 2011–Anticipated completion date for the Florence Tennis Complex (site/courts) and the Tennis Activity Center

The Tennis Center has been a great success over the years. In 2021, it is being expanded and a baseball complex added to accommodate the Florence RedWolves. Brian Parkinon was the first tennis director selected in 2011 and Rob Hill is the current director (as of 2021). The City of Florence provided from their files the following information:

1. Amount of participants in our city tennis leagues:
   - Adults participating in leagues averages around 560 per year with the majority playing on multiple teams
   - Juniors participating in leagues averages around 115 per year with the majority playing on multiple teams
   - Lessons and clinics currently average around 95 tennis instruction hours a week with 120 different participants. There is plenty of demand for us to expand further once we fill our Junior Development Pro position
   - We also offer Junior Summer Camps, 8-week subsidized beginner junior programs, 6-week beginner adult programs, junior UTR match play events, and adult round robins

2. Types of leagues that are offered:
   We offer five separate adult leagues and two junior leagues sanctioned through the United States Tennis Association throughout the year. The list of those leagues are as follows:

   - USTA Spring Adult Leagues
   - USTA Spring Junior Team Tennis Leagues
   - USTA Adult Mixed Doubles Leagues
   - USTA Adult Senior 65 and Over Leagues
   - USTA Adult Combo Doubles Leagues
   - USTA Fall Junior Team Tennis Leagues
   - USTA Adult Tri-Level Leagues

3. Economic impact for the last 3–4 years:

   2018 – $4,313,155
   2019 – $4,166,755

2020 Projected before COVID-19 – $6,325,585
2020 Actual – $1,510,167
2021 Projected – $5,861,611

4. Number of tournaments for the last 3–4 years along with tourna-
    ment schedules:

    2018 – 16 Tournaments
    2019 – 17 Tournaments
    2020 – 10 Tournaments
    2021 – 21 Tournaments

The Basel Group

DEFINITION: a group of six men, Mayor Frank's loyalists that he selected and nurtured, some from the days before his first mayoral race. So named because of their yearly trips to visit Hoffmann-La Roche and other companies in Basel, Switzerland. In order of selection, the group included Fred DuBard, Grady Greer (but prevented from the travels for many years), Dr. Charles Gould, Dr. Stephen Imbeau, Thomas Marschel, and Dr. L. Fred Carter. The real Basel Group included their wives Marguerite, Jessie, Betty, Eleanor, Marilyn, and Folly. Today, the group continues but is diminished: Fred and Jessie have died, as have Betty and Grady; the Goulds have moved to the North Carolina mountains; and the Marschels have drifted away.

Starting several years before Frank ran for mayor, he began to invite community leaders to his apartment for steak suppers every two or three months. With some other equally important advisers, he began afternoon sessions at his construction office. Serious discussions in the early days included the Chamber of Commerce, the All-American City potential, regional cooperation, and downtown redevelopment. These folks included George Jebaily, Ron Chatham, Rick Woodard, Dr. Lee Vickers, Adrian Wilson, Tom Ewart, Robert Williams, Moot Truluck, and Tom Smith. Once elected mayor, Frank decided he needed a core group to be with him through thick and

thin as he faced issues both in and out of Florence. The perfect selection and vetting vehicle was travel: travel out of town to dinner parties with wives, but also to Switzerland to meet with Hoffmann-La
Roche in appreciation for their work in Florence and to make other
business friends in Basel, the Roche headquarters city. And so, the
group of six and Frank were joined to spend time together for business and thoughtful discussion of Florence and to bond together;
these folks become true and cherished friends.

Another place to present some of our project ideas was the quietly
organized Florence Forum. The forum was begun in the late 1970s
by folks from the Florence business community—particularly Joe
Turner and Alan Lewis Sr.—and the real estate community to discuss and help organize development issues in Florence and to make
connections across the community. It became important during
the time Rocky Pearce was mayor. When Frank became mayor, he
became the natural leader and brought several of the Basel Group
folks into the forum; Frank also expanded its membership to include other politicians and leaders from surrounding cities. During
Frank's time, the forum chairs were Robert Williams, Frank Willis,
and Fred DuBard. The forum met at least quarterly, finally in the
private dining room at Francis Marion University when Lee Vickers became president of the university. The forum projects included
several tax referenda for school improvements and roads, regional
development, race relations, and the School Foundation. The forum
came to a natural end by 2004 or so as its numbers had grown too
large, and confidentiality had failed.

Fred DuBard has long played an important but usually quiet role
in the development of Florence. He was important behind the scenes
in the political careers of both Frank Willis and Grady Greer: he was
the quiet but thoughtful adviser, contact man, and the early money.
He and Frank first went to Basel together after a previous trip Frank
made with Herbert Ames (chair, Florence County Council) and Mark
Simmons (executive director, Florence Council County Development
Partnership) a year after Frank made the pioneer trip alone. Russ
Froneberger, a longtime friend of Frank Willis, arranged these first
two trips plus a previous one in 1995 when he, Dr. Bob Henderson,
and Frank went to Zurich, not Basel.

Dr. Charles Gould (of FDTC) joined the travels in 1998 along with Dr. Lee Vickers of FMU. Dr. Gould was the classic university professor with bow tie, a pipe in hand, and the tweed jacket—and very smart. He is one of those folks who can see the future around corners; he also brought educational and administrative experience to the group.

The year 1999 introduced Dr. Stephen A. Imbeau, a local Florence physician who first traveled with the group that year but had attended the earlier steak suppers. Dr. Imbeau brought medical knowledge, entrepreneurship, and a certain ambiance of wonder and adventure to the group, not to mention his travel agent and money skills.

The next year brought Dr. Fred Carter, new president of Francis Marion University. Fred brought to the group his energy, knowledge of South Carolina politics, political skill, and passion for the development of Florence. Two years later, Grady Greer joined the last two trips in 2005 and 2007. He was a successful businessman who had "been there, seen that." He kept our egos in check, but also made sure we reserved proper time for good food and serious discussion. He wanted to make sure our trips had a purpose back home. Tom Marschel, Florence Chamber of Commerce executive and former newspaper publisher, was a longtime member of the group, but could only travel at the end on the 2002, 2003, and 2005 trips; Tom brought important media and Chamber of Commerce connections. Tom's good humor smoothed over our group crankiness when we were tired or stressed.

FRED F. DUBARD was born on May 10, 1935, in Union, South Carolina, and grew up in Chester. He was always the very intelligent guy who made school look easy, but he also liked the streets and people, working early on with his father in the food business, doing odd jobs, and driving a truck.

He graduated from Wofford College with a degree in business and psychology (and eventually became a leader of the Wofford Alumni Association, a *very* important alumni group) and then from the University of Tennessee with a master's degree in educational counseling. As soon as he married Jessie Stanley of Conway on June 7, 1958, Uncle Sam called, but he was assigned to the Army stateside in Knoxville.

After military service, he went with Pearce-Young-Angel (PYA) Company as its sales manager in the Charleston food operation. Moving laterally into the beer business, he was promoted to sales manager with the Budweiser franchise of Greenville. Later, he was made vice president of the Budweiser operation that included Greenville, Spartanburg, Ashville, Anderson, and Columbia.

His rising prominence in the beer business attracted the attention of the Baroody family of Florence. They brought him to Florence in 1972 to be their general manager. His success was astonishing, even to the Baroody family and John Kassab, the president of the N.B. Baroody Beverage Co. In 1989, Fred bought the franchise himself. It was now DuBard Inc. with future business and financial success. He went on to increase sales and become a dominant player in both the Budweiser Company and the National Beer Association.

Fred moved into community service even before buying his business. His first experience was with the Beer Association, both in South Carolina and nationally. Then to community work, beginning with the YMCA, then on to the Florence Monday Rotary Club, the South Carolina Bar Association (lay member on ethics), chair of Coastal Carolina University, Florence-Darlington Technical College Foundation, the North Eastern Strategic Alliance, and the Greater Florence Chamber of Commerce.

Fred developed an easy, intelligent, persuasive style; he would advise rather than command; but once begun, his influence in Florence grew exponentially. He was cool under pressure and rarely seemed rattled or irritated. Tension was often eased with his broad, President Roosevelt-type smile. He preferred to meet folks at his large office desk or on his back porch rocking chairs overlooking The Farm. Fred knew people all around South Carolina. And he put his money where his mouth was.

Fred met Frank through the Rotary Club and economic development. The two developed a deep, lasting friendship. Fred was a key adviser and donator in Frank's early political career and so made a natural ally and partner as Frank organized the Basel Group. Fred died on January 14, 2021. (See "A Hole in My Heart" in *Florence Is Our Home.*)

GRADY L. GREER was born on June 28, 1936, in the family town of Greer, South Carolina. He always had a job, working as a teenager in the same textile plant as his family. He spent four years in the army, stationed in Germany. Then he went to the University of South Carolina in Columbia for several years in a business course. Eventually, he ended up in Darlington, South Carolina, Mayor Frank's town, in about 1960 where two of his four brothers were notable lawyers and businessmen. His family connections, high IQ, and skills landed him a job as assistant district administrator in the Darlington County Schools for the next 11 years. In 1972, Grady joined his brother Jack in the operation of the Toledo Scale franchise in Florence. As his brother moved to retirement, Grady became the manager and then the president and owner of the franchise.

Once Grady had a successful, established business, he plunged into community life. He joined the Florence Monday Rotary Club and over time became one of its leaders, establishing a lifelong bond with Fred DuBard. Eventually, he ran for Florence County Council in 1990 and went on to become chair. He agreed to reorganize the Florence County Economic Development Authority into the Florence County Economic Development Partnership with funding from both government and industry.

He made sure that Frank Willis—an up-and-comer who had attracted Grady's attention while Frank was successful chair of the Florence County Progress and the Authority—be named the new Partnership's first chair. However, Frank decided to run for mayor, and never became chair of the Partnership, resigning from the Authority in early 1995. Grady has left an important legacy in Florence, not only in business but also with the School Foundation. Grady joined the Steak Supper Club early on and eventually traveled with the Basel Group. Grady died on May 27, 2013. (See "A Greer Man" in *Florence Is Our Home*.)

CHARLES "CHARLIE" W. GOULD was born on January 13, 1944, in New York, New York. He started out to be a Jesuit priest but ended up in secular education. He went to college at St. John Vianney College

Seminary in Miami, Florida, from 1959 to 1961 and St. Vincent de Paul Seminary in Boynton Beach, Florida, from 1961 to 1966. He obtained a master's degree in mathematical logic and ethics from the University of Wisconsin in Milwaukee, Wisconsin, (1972–75), and then a doctorate in the philosophy of ethics and religion from Duke University (1975–77). Dr. Gould taught at the University of Wisconsin and Duke University. Along the way, he managed to work for Hi-Time Publishing in Milwaukee as managing editor.

In the early 1980s, he came to work in South Carolina's excellent technical college system and made it his career. When FDTC was looking for a new president in 1993, they brought Dr. Gould up from Georgetown. His impact on Florence was almost immediate. He stabilized the school and prodded it to grow and expand. From early on, he joined the Florence Rotary Club and worked with the Chamber of Commerce. He was smart, clever, great with people, and a visionary; he became the natural leader of any endeavor he joined.

Because he was the college president, he almost immediately met Frank and Fred and nurtured the relationship through the Rotary Club; early on, Frank brought Charlie into the Steak Supper Club. Charlie did not get involved in politics but was always the quiet resource and sounding board in the background. He was an important member of the Basel Group. Charlie was appointed to the Florence County Economic Development Partnership in 1999 and served as chair from 2002 to 2012 with an unparalleled tenure of both duration and impact; Mike Eades and Joe King were his two directors. Several of his successful projects included Heinz, IFH, Otis, Monster, QVC, and Johnson Controls. Probably the most important legacy of his time in Florence will be the SiMT (see "SiMT") at the FDTC campus. He retired in 2013 to move to the mountains of North Carolina.

STEPHEN A. IMBEAU was born on November 25, 1947, on the wrong coast, in Portland, Oregon, growing up in Oakland, California. His parents were told to expect mental retardation since he was born with fetal distress, but they were pleasantly surprised when he met his childhood milestones, some even early. His father was a machinist for the Hyster Company who went on to become a salesman. Steve grew up as a nerd, with absolutely no athletic ability at all; he didn't date until age 19, a junior in college. He attended the University of California at Berkeley to study mathematics and computer science and then medical school at the University of California at San Francisco, graduating with his MD in May 1973. He completed his internship and residency in internal medicine at the University of Wisconsin in 1977 and his Allergy Fellowship in June 1979. Steve married Shirley Ruth Burke of Toronto, Canada, in Toronto on August 17, 1979.

The following February, they left Wisconsin to come to Florence, arriving on March 1, 1980, to three inches of snow, joining Dr. Peter Williams's allergy practice; they have been in Florence ever since. The first five years or so were tumultuous; after a few twists and turns, Steve began his own allergy practice in Florence as the first Board Certified Allergist in the region. His practice grew and grew and grew as he moved from independent practice to the Carolina Health Care Group to the Pee Dee Internal Medicine Group, and then he and Dr. Joseph Moyer founded the Allergy, Asthma & Sinus Center in 1996. In 1984, he became the president of the Florence County Medical Society and joined the Board of the South Carolina Medical Association in 1986, becoming its president in 1998. Steve's early medical mentors in Florence were Drs. Frank Boysia, Hans Habemeir, Bill Hester, and Steve Ross; later, Drs. Bruce White, Eddie Floyd, and Louis Wright also helped his medico-political career.

Steve got involved with the Florence community first through the American Lung Association, the Big Brothers, the local medical review organization (PSRO), then the Florence Symphony, becoming president of the Symphony for six years, first in 1994. At this time, he was on the Florence Chamber of Commerce Board, thus meeting Fred and Charlie. He met Frank through Florence County Progress working as membership director while Frank Willis was chair; Steve later became chair of Florence County Progress himself in 1993. He worked in Frank's first race for mayor and so, with all that plus his connection with Councilman Rick Woodard, he was asked to join the Steak Supper Club and then the Basel Group.

Steve was a bit different than the other group members. He was not a businessman nor a key community leader, but he had enthusiasm, wide knowledge, political interests, travel skills, and intellect.

Believe it or not, he actually made a good fit . . . mostly. For sure he was never a "yes man." Steve and Shirley were particularly delighted to have the Basel Group join their 1998 South Carolina Medical Association presidential inauguration celebration in Charleston, where Mayor Frank was one of the formal speakers.

C. THOMAS MARSCHEL worked with members of the Steak Supper Club and the Basel Group for many years. He was usually unable to travel to Europe with the group, so did not officially join the Basel Group until 2003. He clearly was a leader in Florence, first as publisher of the *Florence Morning News* and then as president of the Florence Chamber of Commerce. The Chamber was waning as he assumed control; in fact, one of the first projects of the Steak Supper Club was to get Tom appointed as Chamber president. He stabilized and rebuilt the organization.

Tom was born in June 1945 in St. Louis, Missouri. He was educated at the University of Missouri as a journalism major and went to get his MBA at the Saint Louis University. He served in Vietnam (1970–71) as a first lieutenant and was awarded a Bronze Star. His life then became the newspaper business, first around St. Louis and then across the country, working for the Journal and Register Company and then the Thomson Newspapers. He became a newspaper "fix-it man" for small- to middle-market newspapers, coming in when revenue or readership started to decline, working in St. Louis, Dallas, and Philadelphia. He did well and was well respected in his business. Tom came to Florence in 1995 as publisher of the *Florence Morning News* with the Thomson Newspapers. He and Marilyn decided they liked Florence and wanted to stay even when his tenure at the *Florence Morning News* ended, so he moved to the Chamber of Commerce in 2000 because the Supper Club thought he was the right man. Tom met the rest of us in the Basel Group, having breakfast with most of us, one by one, in his first month in Florence. He asked to meet some of us even before he moved to town. He and Frank organized our first annual Valentine's dinner, Frank's original idea, in 1998 with reservations and transportation to the Abington Manor in nearby Latta, South Carolina. Tom left the group in 2014.

LUTHER F. "FRED" CARTER moved to Florence as the new president of Francis Marion University in 1999, rescuing the university from adversity. Fred was born on May 30, 1950, in Kenova, West Virginia. He graduated with a BA in political science from the University of Central Florida in 1972. He then came to South Carolina for his MPA in 1976 and PhD in political science at the University of South Carolina in Columbia in 1979. Along the way, he became a colonel in the Marine Corps Reserves. He tucked in service as county administrator for Bamberg County, South Carolina, in 1977. It did not take him long to become the chair of Political Science at the College of Charleston, from 1981 to 1987. Dr. Carter next worked for Governor Carroll Campbell from 1987 to 1991, becoming his senior executive assistant; from the governor's office, he moved to be the executive director of the South Carolina Budget and Control Board, possibly the most powerful department of South Carolina's government, from 1991 to 1999. Interestingly, he served as South Carolina Governor Mark Sanford's chief of staff from 2003 to 2004. Dr. Carter has unique experience. He is a very smart, natural leader who knows how to move people and get things done; he has the skill to scold, comfort, and endear in the same conversation. He "knows" what is going on, knows leaders everywhere, and can direct in an emergency. As a university president, Fred immediately began to work with Frank, Fred, and Charlie and soon was part of the Steak Supper Club, the Florence Forum, and then the Basel Group. From 2000 on, he was a key part of all the projects and continues a significant force in and supporter of Florence.

Beginning in 1998, the Basel Group also developed the tradition of Valentine's dinner with our wives, but with the wives at a special, elegant table served by the men, and each given at evening's end a glorious orchid and a special Valentine's card (well, occasionally the forgetful among us brought Easter cards). Clearly, our wives supported our projects and our time away. When using one of our private homes, the men delegated the Valentine's dinner duties with Tom as head chef, Frank the meat provider, Grady the flowers, Charlie the bread and dessert, Steve the vintner and steward, and the two Freds as the servers and directors; Fred D. and Grady organized the after-dinner entertainment. We met at the homes of Frank, Fred D., and Steve many times; we also used Osbornes, Victors, the Abington Manor, and the Country Club of South Carolina. On occasion, other couples would join us, including Deville and Ron Chatham and Kevin and Mike Miller. Another tradition begun in 2002 was a Christmas Eve morning turkey fry with Bloody Marys or other drinks. The turkeys were first cooked at Grady's place, then later at Fred DuBard's place; Mike Miller, then with the Chamber of Commerce, often joined us. The turkey fries ended in 2015. The Valentine's dinners continue.

Soon after Osbornes, a reception and dinner suite for commercial hire, opened in 2001, Frank and Fred D. arranged for us to meet monthly, usually the first Wednesday evening for cheese, wine, and discussion. A club-type room was developed on the second floor behind the ballroom with lockers, special stuffed chairs, and a fireplace. These meetings died out after a year or two, but Osbornes was where we discussed the Florence Legislative Day, Performing Arts Center, various issues of downtown redevelopment, political campaigns, and the SiMT project. We also met at Osbornes to plan our Basel trips and the Valentine's dinners after the monthly meetings ended.

BASEL GROUP PROJECTS

ALL TOGETHER	MOST OF US	SOME OF US
All-American City	Pee Dee Pride Hockey Team	Coastal Growth Partners (see Imbeau, S. and DuBard, F., *Small Town Entrepreneurs*)
Florence County Legislative Day	Performing Arts Center	IRIX
The School Foundation	NESA	The Trelys Fund
Downtown Florence Development Corporation		The Veterans Park
The Florence Forum		SiMT

The Basel group is named for our trips to Basel. Basel is an important industrial, banking, and cultural city in northern Switzerland at the turn of the Rhine River; it borders Germany and France, and in fact, the local airport, called both the Euro Airport and the Mulhouse Airport, serves all three countries. The major industries are banking, chemicals, and pharmaceuticals. Basel is in the German sector of Switzerland; it is the third-largest city in Switzerland with a population of about 200,000. It is also famous for its museums, art, and music.

The city was founded by the Romans (legend says as early as 30 BC) and named in AD 374. In more modern times, it became a center of the European Guild movement, one of which was the Dye Makers whose original guild building is now the Safran Zunft restaurant; from the dye-making industry arose a large chemical manufacturing base. Basel became a major publishing center since Johann Gutenberg from nearby Mainz had influence in Basel. The Catholic Church also established Basel as an educational center around the famous Erasmus of Rotterdam, who lived many years in Basel, even after the Reformation, and is buried there. Basel houses Switzerland's first zoo. The Bank for International Settlement is in Basel and many private banks operate in the city.

The Roche Company was founded there in 1896. Fritz Hoffmann-La Roche founded a precursor company, "Hoffmann, Traub & Company," in Basel in 1855 to produce chemicals and some pharmaceuticals, using his father's money. When Traub left the company in 1896, it became Hoffmann-La Roche and Company (the "La Roche" comes from Fritz Hoffmann's marriage to Adele La Roche in 1895). Vitamins and vitamin derivatives were its early products. In 1934, it became the first company to mass-produce Vitamin C, calling it Redoxon. But its future was secured when it came out with a new sedative from the benzodiazepine class; Valium and Rohypnol became huge international sellers, bringing in astonishing profits. This money allowed for a long series of acquisitions so that Roche is now international, the third-largest pharmaceutical company in the world. Its key business lines now are cancer drugs, immune treatments, and diagnostics.

Genentech was founded in 1976 in California by UC San Francisco professor Herbert Boyer and businessman Robert Swanson with help from Dr. Boyer's colleagues at UCSF (Michael Bishop and Paul Berg) and at Stanford (Stanley Cohen) to produce the first commercial pharmaceutical products cloned from bacteria (at first antibiotics and insulin). Gentech is one of the Roche portfolio companies since 2009, important since former Genentech executives are key to Roche's International management team ever since Genentech became a leader in cancer and immune therapies. Amusing story: before becoming wealthy, Dr. Boyer, who for a time held the most Genentech stock by an individual, was famous at UC San Francisco for wearing the same shirt all week, meals, and all.

Roche continues to be very profitable; it has not missed a dividend payment for over 30 years. The Roche move to Florence has an interesting history. About 1991, Roche decided to expand in the United States with another site outside Nutley, New Jersey, having both pharmaceutical manufacturing and a process development center, in addition to the one in Basel. The Roche Nutley site selection team, headed by Irwin Lerner, began a search involving 20 potential sites of which Florence was one. Florence was put into the potential site package by an executive of Givaudan fragrances, a Roche company, who had worked in Florence when Givaudan was buying property in Florence; Givaudan was a Roche company until 2000. After less than a year, the search was narrowed to two sites, one near Florence, South Carolina, and one near Richmond, Virginia. The site selection team favored the Virginia site.

The Roche executive team from both Nutley and Basel decided to visit both sites over the winter of 1991–92. The Virginia governor, Douglas Wilder, was about two hours late to the Richmond meeting with Roche and was flatly told that the Roche executives including Hoffmann-La Roche chair Dr. Fritz Gerber, had to leave in just another 30 minutes. On the other hand, at the Florence reception, Governor Carroll Campbell was 30 minutes early—even though in a snowstorm—using four-wheel-drive vehicles to clear the way from Columbia along I-20 to the Bonneau Reception Rooms (the idea to leave early and use the SUVs was that of Campbell staffer Fred Carter). The reception was hosted by Governor Campbell, Senator Hugh Leatherman, Mayor Porter, and Florence County Economic Development Authority chair Frank Willis. Dr. Gerber was impressed with the contrast between the Virginia and South Carolina attitudes; we were later told that that night, he decided on Florence.

After the reception, both South Carolina and Florence felt they had made a favorable impression on Dr. Gerber's team, but continued to aggressively work the deal anyway. Florence Darlington Technical

College sent a small team to Switzerland to inspect the needed equipment to 1) make sure they could train workers to use it, 2) show how aggressive Florence was in pursuing the deal, and 3) guarantee that the workers would be well trained should the facility be built in Florence. Finally, Governor Campbell himself made at least one trip to Basel to meet with the Roche team, enforcing the idea that South Carolina was serious about bringing Roche to Florence—and further, that the State of South Carolina supported the local Florence effort.

Quietly, in 1992, Frank and Michael Barnes organized what they called the "Ready or Not Committee" to get the city and region ready for the Roche entrance, working with the Roche advance man, Ron Chatham. They gathered about 25 folks, mostly local big business managers, for regular meetings to look at local and regional infrastructure, government programs, education, medical services, real estate services, banking services, job training (as noted above), and entertainment venues. The effort was not announced to the public. The group also looked at the potential for regional cooperation and intra-Florence County cooperation between the relevant municipalities and the county. They started to look at metropolitan policy organizations in general, unknowingly laying the groundwork for NESA. Even more than before, Frank's efforts moved him out of the economic development arena into a wider circle of contacts and the world of government and business politics. Most of these folks, if still in Florence, worked with Frank and supported Frank in his subsequent run for mayor.

Roche *did* decide to come to Florence. Construction started in early 1993. The technical center was finished in 1993, the administration building in 1995, the pilot plant in 1996, and the launch plant in 1998. Guy Steenrod was the first local manager, replaced in 1996 by Don Herriott who had been a manager with Syntex Pharmaceuticals, which was purchased by Roche in 1994. Don Herriott's Basel superior, Dr. Jan van Koeveringe, considered the Florence Plant one of the best in his portfolio for both design and production. Dr. van Koeveringe made his first visit, quietly, to Florence in 1995. Later, Don Herriott went on to be an international pharmaceuticals plant manager with seven facilities to manage, part of van Koeveringe's Roche management team. Roche sold its Florence plant in 2016 to

Pantheon Pharmaceuticals, which in 2015 had purchased IRIX Pharmaceuticals of Florence. Roche then left Florence.

Since Frank was so involved in helping to bring Roche to Florence, once mayor he was determined to actually go to Basel, the headquarters city of Roche, to say thank you. He had secured Dr. Jan van Koeveringe's blessing. Dr. van Koeveringe remained an important part of the Basel trips until the final one in 2007; his assistant Michael Richter also became important to the Florence folks. Florence even put in pedestrian markers and lighting across the I-20 Spur at Michael Richter's suggestion.

In 2010, as Roche restructured, Dr. van Koeveringe left Roche and went into a financial consulting business, but later went back into pharma as the president and chair of Senn Chemicals AG (amino acids and peptides) in Dielsdorf, Switzerland. Don Herriott also retired from Roche in 2010 and now with his son owns several small restaurants and shops featuring microbrewery beer and a fitness center in the Anderson-Greenwood, South Carolina, area.

Frank never dreamed where his first Swiss trip in 1995 would lead.

THE TRIP YEARS

1995	Frank Willis, Bob Henderson, Russ Froneberger (to Zurich, not Basel)	sf = $1.18
1996	Frank Willis, Russ Froneberger, Mark Simmons, Herbert Ames	sf = $1.24
1997	Frank Willis, Fred DuBard, Russ Froneberger (Eve then helped Russ)	sf = $1.45
1998	Frank Willis, Fred DuBard, Charles Gould, Lee Vickers (the first Eve Martini trip)	sf = $1.50
1999	Frank Willis, Fred DuBard, Charles Gould, Stephen Imbeau	sf = $1.60
2000	Frank Willis, Fred DuBard, Charles Gould, Stephen Imbeau, Adrian Wilson	sf = $1.69
2001	Frank Willis, Fred DuBard, Charles Gould, Stephen Imbeau, Fred Carter	sf = $1.69
2002	Frank Willis, Fred DuBard, Charles Gould, Stephen Imbeau, Tom Marschel	sf = $1.56
2003	Frank Willis, Charles Gould, Stephen Imbeau, Fred Carter, Tom Marschel	sf = $1.35
2005	Frank Willis, Fred DuBard, Charles Gould, Stephen Imbeau, Fred Carter, Tom Marschel, Grady Greer	sf = $1.25
2007	Frank Willis, Fred DuBard, Charles Gould, Stephen Imbeau, Fred Carter, Grady Greer (no Eve Martini)	sf = $1.20

THE WILD BUNCH

Russ Froneberger has been a longtime friend of Frank's, moving from the banking world to the economic development and foreign contact world as a consultant and adviser. He now lives in Blufton, South Carolina, near Hilton Head. He organized Frank's first trip to Zurich and the first two trips to Basel.

We picked Eve Martini-Pawlik up from Russ Froneberger. She had worked as a secretary and assistant to Dr. Hans Vauthier in Ciba Geigy, and then for Russ Froneberger. She lives near Basel and still works with Russ's Global Consultants but calls her own business "World Wide Links." She planned each day of our trips, except for our free time and special evenings. She organized our meetings each day, our luncheons, and our dinners. She met us at the hotel each morning and often took us in her own car. As our group expanded, we often rented a second car from the hotel, or she provided a van.

On his first trip to Europe as mayor of Florence, Frank actually did not make it to Basel. Russ Froneberger asked Frank to come with him to Zurich in 1995, along with Dr. Bob Henderson, CEO of the South Carolina Research Authority, after Frank had been elected. But they did not get to Basel, Frank's real objective. So, in 1996, Frank asked Russ to organize a trip for him to Basel along with Herbert Ames (chair of Florence County Council) and Mark Simmons (executive director of the Florence County Economic Development Partnership). They met with the Roche executives and Frank did say thank you face-to-face. Frank was surprised when they told him no city had ever come to headquarters to say thank you, and so he decided to further develop the relationship with future trips. Frank's group met with Roche executives Fritz Gerber, Franz Humen, Kurt Hausman, and Dr. Jan van Koeveringe and had dinner with them. A relationship was begun. Frank's group also had a delightful dinner at the private home of Christoph Gruenfelder of the Basel Economic Development offices.

The next year, Russ arranged a similar trip to Basel; Frank was accompanied by Fred DuBard. They visited with the Chamber of Commerce and Basel Economic Development and toured the Feldschlossen Brewery, the airport (meeting airport director Paul Rhinow), and went over to ABB in Zurich.

The next trip was in 1998 and Dr. Charles Gould and Dr. Lee Vickers (president of FMU) came along to join Frank and Fred DuBard. This trip was the first one arranged by Eve Martini. During this trip, Fred and Dr. Gould discovered the #11 tram to Aesch, and there made friends with the local Harley-Davison dealer, John Richards, who once lived in the United States; amusingly, his logo says, "Our legend grows." Dr. Gould was a motorcyclist and in particular a Harley man; he and Fred DuBard usually bought some small item and had coffee with John. During this trip, the group started the tradition of going to Chez Donati for veal on Saturday night and Restaurant Stucki for dinner on Wednesday night. Chez Donati was so excellent that in 2005 Steve got up from his deathbed to join for dinner but could only have soup. On the first visit to Donati's in 1998, Dr. Gould discovered they accepted only checks or cash; so, he negotiated to pay them later from the United States by check. They agreed, he did, and we have gone back to Donati's every trip since.

Restaurant Stucki (owned since 1997 by Pierre Buess and served by Chef Zimmermann, and called the Restaurant Bruderholz, but still "Stucki" to the locals) became our second favorite Basel restaurant. Unfortunately, Restaurant Stucki is under new ownership since 2008, and much changed from its former European cuisine. The airport director, Paul Rhinow, was close to the Stucki family and in 2000 he reintroduced us all to Susi, the widow of the Grand Chef Hans Stucki, at their namesake restaurant over complimentary cocktails and appetizers (no discount on the meal, however). For twenty years, she and her husband lived above their restaurant in a beautiful home on the Bruderholz. Fred and Frank had first gone to Restaurant Stucki in 1997 and met with both the Stuckis just before Chef Hans died; in fact, Hans came by their table to chat that first night.

Frank and Fred DuBard had met executives of the Bank Sarasin, Philip Baumann, and Georg Kroyer, in 1997 and 1998 at the Rotary St. Jakob; at that time, Frank was asked to speak at Rotary next time in Basel. In 2000, he gave a presentation about Florence and why we were in Basel, and the local chair gave a talk about Rotary membership.

In 2000, Canton Basel-Stadt President Carlo Conti introduced us all around to the local dignitaries and some business leaders. Mayor Willis of course was our headliner and toastmaster for Florence.

Fine China and silver in a long Canton Hall third floor. A night to remember.

The University of Basel is the oldest in Switzerland, founded in 1460. It is self-governed although under the jurisdiction of the Cantons of Basel-Stadt and Basel-Land. It is home to 3,500 staff, 1,700 faculty, and 13,000 students. Its annual budget is approximately 500 million Swiss francs, of which one-fourth each is borne by the two sponsoring Cantons. The remaining costs are covered through federal contributions, third-party funding, other cantons, and tuition fees; tuition is about $800 per semester. It ranks in the top ten among German-speaking universities. It has a close relationship with Novartis.

We visited three or four times. The University of Basel and Florence Darlington Technical College have an exchange relationship. One time, we had a nice reception with students from Florence and some of their new Swiss friends at the university. Dr. Gould had some private meetings with university staff. The rest of us were impressed with the huge number of bicycles around the campus.

WEHR

Wehr is a small industrial town in Germany near Bad Säckingen founded in 1902. We visited three businesses there; one, a tool and die company called Visuelle- Medien; one, an adhesive company; and one, a lighting company called Moon Light. We met with the mayor on one of the trips, Michael Thater. The business visits followed a set pattern: a tour of the plant, usually *not* brief, then a lecture about the business with some "takeaway" literature, and then some refreshments which were almost always Coca-Cola, bottled water, and cookies.

BAD SÄCKINGEN

Bad Säckingen is a spa and medical German town dating back to the Middle Ages, famous even during the time of Erasmus as a medical facility for its mineral springs and waters. A large hospital and clinic have built up around the spa in modern times. It was the setting for a famous nineteenth-century German novel, *The Trumpeter of*

Säckingen, and the town still promotes that history. Since it sits on the Rhine, it has at least one famous covered bridge between it and Switzerland.

Mayor Gunther Nufer was trained as a lawyer; he worked his political way up in the Social Democratic Party in Hamburg, Bonn, Freiburg, and Stuttgart. He was sent to run for mayor of Bad Säckingen by the party leadership in 1971 and won with over 70 percent of the vote. The city had fallen on hard times, and he revived it by enhancing the Spa, then creating around it a clinic emphasizing rehabilitation, and then a hospital; he was adept at both fundraising and getting federal government support. He developed relationships for the clinic with surrounding universities. As the federal government changed parties in the 1980s, he continued winning reelections by wide margins.

Mayor Nufer became an entrepreneur once the city was financially sound. He developed support businesses for the clinic and its patients: motel and apartments and an RV center, a physical therapy school, a massage therapy school, and even a golf course called Hochreheim, of which he remains the president. He proudly showed us them all. He stays active as president of the Hochreheim golf world, director of his schools, and helps to run his own charitable foundation.

Our first visit to Bad Säckingen in 2001 was because of the clinic. The clinic administration gave us a tour of the emergency room, the X-ray department, the orthopedic department, and the rehabilitation department. Over lunch in one of their conference rooms, they gave us a special presentation on wound healing based on research they were doing with diet and oxygen therapy. We call it "Dr. Nufer's Clinic" because he has been awarded an honorary doctorate.

On our 2002 trip, Nufer scheduled a press conference with TV and print press for Mayor Willis and himself. It took place at Bad Säckingen city hall.

Darlington County Economic Development Partnership

COMING OUT of retirement beginning on July 2, 2012, Frank became executive director of the Darlington County Economic Development Partnership, previously the Darlington County Economic Development Authority. It was a natural fit. Frank grew up in Darlington County, he had construction, political, and governmental experience. He had contacts all around the region, state, nation, and world. To boot, economic development was always part of his platform as mayor. He knew the economic development world.

He told the newspapers at the time, "I know the people, I know the place, and I've always loved economic development, just find it interesting. And I'm going home here at the end of my career" (*Morning News*, June 29, 2012).

But even the year before he began formal work, he worked with the county to reconfigure their economic development activities cumulating in the development of the new Partnership by local legislation on November 7, 2011. Darlington County Progress was the private sector organization previously developed to promote and assist the Authority. The change was not only in name but also in structure: the Partnership executive director would report directly to the county administrator rather than the Progress director; Dale Surrett was the county administrator at the time. The Partnership mission statement read, "The Partnership was established to improve the economy of Darlington County through the effective promotion and development of new industry and the expansion of existing industry. The Partnership is responsible for working with state and federal agencies in securing available grants and other financial assistance for industries." The original members of the new Partnership board included Frank as acting director with Barry Tayler, Leo Bonaparte, J. Lewis Brown (current executive director as of 2021), Gregory Alexander, Roger Buckley, James Ivey Jr., Ryan Nettles, Donald Clark, Danny Hogge Jr., (on staff), Doyle Hopper (on staff), Stewart Ames and Jeff Singletary. The Darlington County Economic Development Partnership became famous under Frank for its snappy newsletter.

Curiously, there was a continuing Darlington County relationship with Florence at the time. Tommy Edwards, former administrator of both the City of Florence and the County of Florence, became Darlington's county administrator from July 2010 until January 2011. He resumed that role in August 2014. Frank served in that same role for several months between Dale Surrett and Tommy Edwards.

Frank moved the Authority offices to the campus of the Florence Darlington Technical College in order to be on Darlington property— since the college was operated and funded jointly between the two counties—and to be close to the regional hub of Florence and to provide more "juice" to the SiMT complex on the FDTC campus. He opened the offices at the SiMT incubator on the FDTC campus at 1951 Pisgah Road, #120.

A major Darlington County project during Frank's tenure was the rebirth of the Wellman Palmetto Plant on McIver Road as the newest Fiber Industries plant. Facing internal strife and financing problems, Wellman was forced into bankruptcy in 2008. The Palmetto Plant at its peak employed over a thousand people and produced about 225,000 metric tons of polyester staple per year. In 2009, the plant and property of about 765 acres with a rail spur were picked up by Industrial Process Plants (IPP) of New Jersey, using an entity called Darlington Development. IPP is a world-leading source of second-hand plants & process equipment. In 2013, MHR Fund Management of New York, a hedge fund started by Mark Rachesky in 1996 that had become a $5 billion fund, entered into a financing agreement with IPP regarding several plants IPP owned.

In the second half of 2016, MHR determined that the business plan put forth by Andrew Rosenfeld and Leandro Carboni warranted investment and the two of them would become the executives of Fiber Industries. All four parties finalized the agreements and formed Fiber Industries in April 2017. During this time, the State of South Carolina was able to input job development credits through the Coordinating Council of Economic Development (Governor Henry McMaster and Secretary of Commerce Bobby Hitt) and Darlington County (chair Bobby Hudson) providing fees in lieu of taxes and some grant monies.

Andrew Rosenfeld took on the public face of the new company; he earned a BS in chemicals and petroleum-refining engineering from the Colorado School of Mines and an MBA in finance from American University, having work experience with Marathon Petroleum and Koch Industries, then into the world of finance at Schroder and Co, Prudential, Impala Asset Management (as a managing director and investor), and Citadel.

The new business owners invested over $30 million of capital and repaired and replaced equipment and infrastructure on the site as needed along with new and sophisticated management, accounting, and communications software using cloud technology. They hired over 180 people to run the 1.1-million-square-foot facility and in 2020 started producing high-quality polyester staple fiber with many commercial and consumer uses. About 80 percent of their customers are within two hundred miles of the plant.

———————

Frank was succeeded in February 2021 by director Lewis Brown, recently retired from Sonoco and a past member of both the Authority and the Darlington County Council.

Historical and editorial assistance came from Andrew Rosenfeld.

APPENDIX

Pee Dee Pride Hockey Team

From Wikipedia:

The Pee Dee Pride, known as the Florence Pride for the 2003–04 ECHL season, were a professional minor-league hockey team that was based in Florence, South Carolina, where they played in the East Coast Hockey League (ECHL) from 1997 until 2005. The team came to Florence as a relocation of the Knoxville Cherokees, one of the five charter members of the ECHL which was originally housed in Knoxville, Tennessee [and owned by an investor group headed by Hayes Payne].

The Pride played at the Florence Civic Center, which seats 7,426 fans. The name of the organization comes from the region of South Carolina in which Florence is located, known as the "Pee Dee" region. The team's mascot was Paws the Lion. The organization never won the Kelly Cup, the ECHL championship trophy. However, the Pride were previous winners of the Palmetto Cup for best team in South Carolina, and the Brabham Cup for best regular season record. In-state rivals of the Pride included the South Carolina Stingrays, the Greenville Grrrowl, and the Columbia Inferno.

[Reports have circulated that the owners attempted to relocate the team to Myrtle Beach, South Carolina.] However, construction on a planned 7,000-seat arena on the campus of Coastal Carolina University

stalled. Finally, at the ECHL league meetings in June 2009, the franchise
was returned to the league, ending its lineage.

The team was purchased by a Florence ownership group called
Florence Hockey in 2002 with partners Fred DuBard, Stephen Imbeau, Debbie Hyler, Marguerite Willis, Hugh Leatherman, and Frank
Avent. In 2004, Willis, Leatherman, and Avent surrendered their
ownership interest. Jack Capuano was the general manager from
1999; Debbie Hyler came on as the chief operating officer in 2003.
Fred DuBard was the managing partner.

From Wikipedia:

Jack Capuano (born July 7, 1966 [in Cranston, Rhode Island]) is . . .
a former head coach of the New York Islanders . . . Capuano played as
a defenseman and spent parts of three seasons in the NHL in the late
1980s and early 1990s. He is the brother of former NHL hockey player
Dave Capuano.

Capuano played high school hockey at the Kent School in Kent, Con-
necticut and was a 5th round selection (88th overall) in the 1984 NHL
Entry Draft. He played his college hockey at the University of Maine.
At Maine, he was a teammate of his younger brother Dave Capuano
and played on the same blueline as future NHLers Eric Weinrich and
Bob Beers along with future Toronto Maple Leafs General Manager,
Dave Nonis. He enjoyed a decorated college career, earning First-Team
All-American honors in his junior year. His 32 goals remains the most
ever by a Black Bear defenseman.

YEARLY STANDINGS

SEASON	TEAM	LEAGUE	DIVISION	GP	W	L	T	OTL
1997–98	Pee Dee Pride	ECHL	Southeast	70	34	25	0	0
1998–99	Pee Dee Pride	ECHL	Southeast	70	51	15	0	0
1999–00	Pee Dee Pride	ECHL	Southeast	70	47	18	0	0
2000–01	Pee Dee Pride	ECHL	Southeast	72	38	28	0	0
2001–02	Pee Dee Pride	ECHL	Southeast	72	41	25	0	0
2002–03	Pee Dee Pride	ECHL	Southeast	72	40	26	0	0
2003–04	Florence Pride	ECHL	Southern	72	30	33	0	0
2004–05	Pee Dee Pride	ECHL	East	72	31	36	0	2

Capuano turned pro in 1988 following his junior year and signed with the Maple Leafs. He spent his first season with the Newmarket Saints of the AHL recording 21 points in 74 games. He would crack the Leafs' NHL roster for the 1989–90 season, but played in only 1 game before Tom Kurvers returned from a holdout, forcing his demotion. Shortly after his demotion, he walked out on the Saints and demanded a trade, feeling he belonged in the NHL.

Toronto would deal Capuano to the New York Islanders mid-season, but they too assigned him to the AHL. He played only 17 games in the Islanders' system before being dealt again, this time to the Vancouver Canucks.

Capuano would have his finest professional season in 1990–91, recording 20 goals and 50 points and earning 2nd-team All-Star honors in the IHL playing for the Milwaukee Admirals, Vancouver's minor-pro affiliate. He received a three-game callup to the Canucks, where he received the opportunity to play with his brother Dave. The two became the first pair of brothers in Canucks history to suit up for the team at the same time.

Capuano signed as a free agent with the Boston Bruins for the 1991–92 season. He enjoyed another solid season in the AHL, and another two games of NHL action with the Bruins, but chose to retire at the end of the season. He finished his career having appeared in 6 NHL games without recording a point.

Following his career as a player, Capuano moved into coaching. He served as an assistant coach with the Tallahassee Tiger Sharks of the ECHL before being hired as head coach of the ECHL's Pee Dee Pride in

SOL	PTS	PCT	GF	GA	PIM	ATTEN.	COACH
11	76	0.564	214	215	1578	5355	Jack Capuano
4	106	0.757	289	191	1674	5719	Jack Capuano
5	99	0.707	233	175	1329	5165	Frank Anzalone
6	82	0.569	242	231	1390	4013	Anzalone, Payne {+}
6	88	0.611	236	218	1495	3338	Davis Payne
6	86	0.597	244	213	1633	2991	Davis Payne
9	69	0.479	210	254	1248	2505	Perry Florio
3	67	0.465	203	219	1409	2660	Perry Florio

1997 and added the GM title to his responsibilities a year later. He left
the bench in 1999 but continued as GM until 2005, when the franchise
folded.

Capuano then signed on to be an assistant coach for the New York
Islanders in the 2005–06 season. The team played fairly well, despite
a midseason coaching change, but failed to make the playoffs. The following season, 2006–07, Capuano became an assistant coach for the
Islanders' AHL affiliate, the Bridgeport Sound Tigers. On April 30, 2007,
Capuano was named head coach of the Sound Tigers for the 2007–2008
season.

On November 15, 2010, Capuano was named interim head coach of
the Islanders after head coach Scott Gordon was fired from that position by GM Garth Snow amidst a 10-game losing streak by the team.
The Islanders retained Capuano as the full-time coach for the 2011–12
season. Capuano led the Islanders to a playoff spot in 2013, their first
appearance in six years.

Jack worked as the New York Islanders coach until 2017 with a
salary of about $2 million per year (a lot more than the $65,000 per
year paid by the Pride). He now is an assistant coach with the Ottawa
Senators. The USA Hockey newsletter recently highlighted his work
with the International Ice Hockey Federation (IIHF):

> Jack Capuano, who is currently serving as associate coach with the
> Ottawa Senators, will be representing the U.S. [in the IIHF Men's World
> Championship] as a coach for the fourth time. He served as an assistant
> coach for Team USA at the 2017 IIHF Men's World Championship and at
> the 2016 World Cup of Hockey, and was the head coach of the 2005 U.S.
> Under-18 Select Team at the Five Nations Cup in Slovakia. In addition
> to his time in Ottawa, Capuano's 25-year professional hockey career
> has included time in the ECHL, AHL and NHL, including as head coach
> of the New York Islanders from 2010–17. He has also had stops with the
> Florida Panthers, Bridgeport Sound Tigers, Pee Dee Pride, Knoxville
> Cherokee and Tallahassee Tiger Sharks, where he began his post-play-
> ing days hockey career as an assistant coach.

Senator Hugh Leatherman

HUGH K. LEATHERMAN was elected to the South Carolina Senate on November 4, 1980.

Hugh was born and raised on a farm in Lincoln County, North Carolina, where at a very early age he learned the value of a hard day's work. After graduating from the area's public high school, he enrolled at North Carolina State University. During his time at NC State, he learned the importance of science and mathematics, where he graduated with a Bachelor of Science in civil engineering. Following the completion of college, Hugh moved to Florence.

Hugh began his career in public service in 1967 when he was elected to the Quinby Town Council. From 1971 to 1976, Hugh served as mayor pro tempore of the Town of Quinby.

Through his service in local and state office, Hugh is a valuable asset to the entire Pee Dee region, as he has served the Florence area for more than 30 years. Currently, Hugh serves as chair of the powerful Senate Finance Committee, while also serving on the Senate Ethics, Interstate Cooperation, Labor, Commerce and Industry, Rules, State House, and Transportation Committees. Also, Hugh serves as one of the five members of the State Fiscal Accountability Authority, which oversees the state's financial dealings on a monthly basis. He also serves on the South Carolina Research Authority board of directors. In each of these positions, Hugh has been very influential in securing various state funds for many infrastructure and economic development projects throughout the entire Pee Dee region— projects that are vital to the community.

Hugh was elected president pro tempore of the South Carolina Senate on June 18, 2014.

For his many years of leadership, service, and dedication to the people of the Pee Dee region and the entire state of South Carolina, numerous organizations and institutions have graciously honored him. Most notably, he has received an honorary doctorate from Francis Marion University, the College of Charleston, the Medical University of South Carolina, the Citadel, Coastal Carolina University, the University of South Carolina, Clemson University, Lander University, South Carolina State University, Wofford College, and Winthrop University.

Hugh is married to Jean Leatherman, and he has six children and six grandchildren. Senator and Mrs. Leatherman are members of Central United Methodist Church in Florence.

City of Florence Officials

MAYOR FRANK was fortunate to work with a stable city government.

City manager: Tommy Edwards until May 1996, Edward Burchins (for 11 months), then David N. Williams beginning in June 1997.

Public Works and Utilities: Andrew "Drew" Griffin

City council members: J. Ray Turner, Ben Dozier, John Chase, Billy D. Williams, Edward Robinson, Maitland S. Chase, Bill Bradham, Bobby Holland, Rick Woodard, and Buddy Brand

FLORENCE COUNTY ECONOMIC DEVELOPMENT AUTHORITY/ PARTNERSHIP, DIRECTORS	
Curt Hogan	1988–90
Frank Willis	1990–91 (acting)
Michael Barnes	1991–95
Mark Simmons	1995–97
Brent McMahon	1997–98
Trish Caulder	1998–2000 (acting)
Jack Michael Eades	2000–03
Joe King	2003–

About the Authors

STEPHEN A. IMBEAU was born on November 25, 1947, on the wrong coast, in Portland, Oregon, growing up in Oakland, California. His parents were told to expect mental retardation since he was born with severe fetal distress, but they were pleasantly surprised when he met the childhood milestones, some even early. His father was a machinist for the Hyster Company, a subsidiary of the Caterpillar Company, and went on to become a salesman.

Imbeau grew up as a nerd, with absolutely no athletic ability at all, not dating until age 19, a junior in college. He attended college at the University of California at Berkeley in mathematics and computer science and then medical school at the University of California at San Francisco, graduating with a Doctor of Medicine degree in May of 1973. He completed both internship and residency in Internal medicine at the University of Wisconsin in 1977 and Allergy Fellowship in June 1979.

He married Shirley Ruth Burke of Toronto, Canada, in Toronto on August 18, 1979. In February, they left Wisconsin to come to Florence, arriving March 1, 1980, to three inches of snow, joining Dr. Peter Williams allergy practice. The first five years or so were tumultuous; after a few twists and turns, Imbeau began his own allergy practice in Florence as the first Board Certified Allergist in the region. The practice grew and grew and grew as he moved from independent practice to the Carolina Health Care Group to the Pee Dee Internal Medicine Group, and then with Dr. Joseph Moyer founded the Allergy, Asthma & Sinus Center in 1996.

In 1984, he became the president of the Florence County Medical Society and joined the board of the South Carolina Medical Association in 1986, becoming its president in 1998. Early medical mentors in Florence included Drs. Frank Boysia, Hans Habemeir, Bill Hester, and Steve Ross; later Drs. Bruce White, Eddie Floyd, and Louis Wright also helped his medico-political career.

He got involved with the Florence Community first through the American Lung Association, the Big Brothers, the local medical review organization (PSRO), then the Florence Symphony, becoming president of the Symphony for six years, first in 1994. He joined the Chamber of Commerce Board and the Florence County Progress becoming chairman of County Progress in 1993. He became active in Mayor Frank Willis' campaign and worked closely with the mayor throughout his term and beyond.

He also developed a career at the American Medical Association (AMA), becoming alternate delegate to the AMA from South Carolina in 1996. He left South Carolina for a time to work at AMA with the American Academy of Allergy, Asthma, and Immunology, return-

ing to the South Carolina Delegation at AMA in 2004. He became chair of the South Carolina Delegation in 2007 until 2015. In 2013, he became chairman of the Southeastern Delegation to AMA for two years; also, in 2011 he became Chair of the Elections Committee, and editor of the SED Newsletter in 2011, both offices continuing. He is also now the Chair of the American Medical Political Action Committee.

For more about Stephen and his writing, please visit *stephenaimbeau.com.*

FRANK E. WILLIS was born on October 19, 1941, in Bennettsville, South Carolina. He grew up in Darlington, South Carolina, and was athletic and sports minded. He graduated from the University of South Carolina in Columbia in 1964 with a bachelor's degree in psychology. Frank came back home to work in his father's construction business; a portrait of his father hung in his office until the business was sold. As owner and CEO of Willis Construction Company, headquartered in Florence, South Carolina, Frank became successful. He volunteered in his trade association, and in 1980 helped establish the South Carolina Transportation Policy and Research Council. Later, he became active locally, appointed to the Florence County Progress organization and moved up to be its chair in 1989. Frank became the chair of the Florence County Economic Development Authority in 1991. His economic development work attracted the attention and friendship of Fred DuBard and Grady Greer. Grady was chair of the Florence County Council and Fred was involved with the Rotary Club, Florence Chamber of Commerce, and a true "behind the scenes" leader of Florence. The Rotary Club at that time was key to the traditional leadership of Florence. As Frank became prominent in the economic development arena, he gained political confidence and a wide circle of important contacts, and so decided to run for mayor of Florence.

Acknowledgments

WE WISH to thank Drs. Carter and Gould and Thomas Marschel for the shared experiences, their enormous contributions to Florence, and their invaluable help in the writing of this book. We value the memory and contributions of Grady Greer, Barbara Sylvester, and Fred DuBard. We deeply appreciate the years of service and friendship of George Jebaily. We thank all our other helpers in the writing of this book, in no particular order: Senator Hugh Leatherman, David Williams, Drew Griffin, Pam Osborne, George Jebaily, Jeff McKay, Amanda Pope, Anson Shells, Martha Ray, and David Brown.

Frank thanks all his supporters in his election campaigns and key projects. Frank wishes to thank his city council members and staff at the City of Florence during his term and a particular thanks to David Williams and Drew Griffin. Frank also wants to thank all the dedicated citizens of Florence who worked on the projects delineated in this book, numbering in the hundreds and far too many to thank individually, but oh so much loved and appreciated. We also wish to thank Austin Gilbert for his photographic labor of love. We thank all the citizens of Florence for all their work and support along the way.

A special thanks to Marguerite Willis, for her enthusiastic and warm and loyal love of Frank.

We thank the Credo Communications group for their invaluable assistance to make this book possible: Tim Beals, Pete Ford, and Sharon VanLoozenoord. Well done.

To Chad Allen, book consultant, continued thanks.

And to you, our readers—*thanks.*

Frank Willis and Stephen Imbeau, 2021

Photo Credits

Businessman

The Darlington Raceway, actionsports, depositphotos
Florence County Economic Development Authority datasheet, Shirley Imbeau
Willis Construction office, Stephen Imbeau
Honda South Carolina, *Morning News-SCNow*
Conway Bypass, Chris Reid and Dan Garnell, gribblenation.com
Roche Carolina site, siteselection.com

The Campaigns

Mailer, Barbara Sylvester, Frank Willis, and Pam Osborn
Brochure, Barbara Sylvester, Frank Willis, and Pam Osborn
Bumper sticker, Barbara Sylvester, Frank Willis, and Pam Osborn
Inauguration (2), James Schofield

Drug Free Florence

Church Street lot, Stephen Imbeau
All-American City and Community Award Campaign
Application, Shirley Imbeau
Bumper Sticker, Stephen Imbeau
Tom Kinard and Jane Pigg on the radio, from the "Kinard 'N Koffee" show archives
Spoof, Stephen Imbeau, taken from the Wingard Family Collection

Preventing Juvenile Crime

McLeod Park skate park (2), Stephen Imbeau

The Veterans Park

Entrance, Austin Gilbert

Dedication Day programs, Barry Wingard

Dedication ceremony, Barry Wingard

All internal park pictures (11), Austin Gilbert

Visions 2010

Hotel Florence, Stephen Imbeau

FDTC campus, Stephen Imbeau

Restaurant Row, Stephen Imbeau

Florence County Legislative Day

Columbia Museum of Art, Stephen Imbeau

Passport, Stephen Imbeau

Legislative Day gifts (5), Stephen Imbeau

SiMT

Brochure, Ed Bethea and Jill Lewis, FDTC Collection

Fountain, Ed Bethea and Jill Lewis, FDTC Collection

Pop-up, Ed Bethea and Jill Lewis, FDTC Collection

Extension, Ed Bethea and Jill Lewis, FDTC Collection

NESA

NESA logo, nesasc.org

Early days, Stephen Imbeau

New location, Stephen Imbeau

Infrastructure: Water and Sewer

Water and sewer master plan, Stephen Imbeau

Wastewater management facility, Stephen Imbeau

Water treatment plant, Stephen Imbeau

Infrastructure: Downtown Florence

Downtown revitalization map, Hunter Interests

Hunter Interests brochure, Hunter Interests

Drs. Bruce and Lee Library, Brad Callicott

Florence County Museum, flocomuseum.org, museum staff, and the files of George Jebaily

Florence City Center, Stephen Imbeau

Rebuilt Downtown Florence, Ray Reich, FDDC, onlyinyourstate.com

Little Theatre, Little Theatre staff and the files of John Bankson, florencelittletheatre.org

James Allen Plaza, Stephen Imbeau

Drs. Bruce and Lee Foundation original board photo, Bradley Callicott, the Drs. Bruce and Lee Foundation

The Performing Arts Center

Posters (2), FMU Collection, Beverly Hazelwood and Shirley Imbeau

Performing Arts Center, Stephen Imbeau

Brochure, FMU Collection,

Plaque, Stephen Imbeau

The School Foundation
> The School Foundation logo, Debbie Hyler of the School Foundation

The Dr. Eddie Floyd Florence Tennis Complex
> Entrance, Stephen Imbeau
> Jennie O'Bryan Avenue sign, Stephen Imbeau
> Tennis courts, Stephen Imbeau
> Tennis Center building, Stephen Imbeau

The Basel Group
> Basel Group, Shirley Imbeau
> Basel Group wives (3), Shirley Imbeau
> Map, fr.weather-forecast.com
> Tram map, Pinterest
> Restaurant Stucki, Stephen Imbeau
> Tinguely Fountain, Stephen Imbeau
> Willi's Cafe, Stephen Imbeau
> On location, Eve Martini
> Basel City Hall, Stephen Imbeau
> Novartis, Novartis
> Roche, Roche web page
> Students, Eve Martini
> Nufer Clinic, Karl Barun, Michael Rohrer, and Florian Adler, *Bad Säckingen*,
>   G. Braun Buchverlag, 2001
> Mayor Nufer, *Badische Zeitung*
> Two mayors, Mayor Nufer's press photographer

Darlington County Economic Development Partnership
> SiMT, Shirley Imbeau
> Darlington Economic Development office, Shirley Imbeau
> Fiber Industries logo, fiberindusties.com
> Fiber Industries plant, Andrew Rosenfeld, IDL

Appendix
> Florence Center, weddingwire.com
> Jersey, Stephen Imbeau
> Pride logo, Stephen Imbeau
> Sign, Stephen Imbeau
> Christmas card, Debbie Hyler
> Senator Hugh Leatherman, the senator and his staff

Printed in the USA
CPSIA information can be obtained
at www.ICGtesting.com
LVHW071331050124
768178LV00009B/109

9 781625 862075